daybook, *n.* a book
in which the events
of the day are
recorded; *specif.* a
journal or diary

DAYBOOK
of Critical Reading and Writing

FRAN CLAGGETT

LOUANN REID

RUTH VINZ

Great Source Education Group
a Houghton Mifflin Company
Wilmington, Massachusetts

www.greatsource.com

The Authors

Fran Claggett, currently an educational consultant for schools throughout the country and teacher at Sonoma State University, taught high school English for more than thirty years. She is author of several books, including *Drawing Your Own Conclusions: Graphic Strategies for Reading, Writing, and Thinking* (1992) and *A Measure of Success* (1996).

Louann Reid taught junior and senior high school English, speech, and drama for nineteen years and currently teaches courses for future English teachers at Colorado State University. Author of numerous articles and chapters, her first books were *Learning the Landscape* and *Recasting the Text* with Fran Claggett and Ruth Vinz (1996).

Ruth Vinz, currently a professor and director of English education at Teachers College, Columbia University, taught in secondary schools for twenty-three years. She is author of several books and numerous articles that discuss teaching and learning in the English classroom as well as a frequent presenter, consultant, and co-teacher in schools throughout the country.

TABLE OF CONTENTS

3

4

7

Angles of Literacy: Reading Anne Sexton's Poetry

There are many ways to read a novel or poem, just as there are many ways to look at the world. We talk about reading the weather, other people's moods, a friend's actions, or a parent's tone of voice. This kind of reading may not be the same thing you think of when your teacher assigns you a story, poem, or novel, but it requires the same kind of thinking on your part.

As you look at a work from a number of different angles, you will find new ways of understanding it. A literary work is like a fabric of many colors or textures. Each reader takes a different thread or color of meaning from what is said and unsaid. The meaning of what you read is between you and the text.

The angles of literacy— interacting with the text, making connections to other things you have read and experienced, shifting perspectives, analyzing the author's language and craft, and examining how an author's life and work are interrelated—will help you focus your reading. By looking at literature from these angles, you will become both a more perceptive reader and a more imaginative one.

Some of the strategies readers use to interact with a text are to underline, write questions, and make notes in the margin about ideas they agree with or disagree with. They use the margin to carry on a kind of dialogue with the author. As a model of how to annotate text, here are the notations one reader made on a first reading of Anne Sexton's poem "To a Friend Whose Work Has Come to Triumph."

Response notes

verbs order the reader

great image of the sun

10

his father cares

I still don't completely understand the title, but I'm getting an idea that the author thinks that flying into the sun and falling isn't such a bad way to go. Icarus is "wondrously tunneling" and "acclaiming the sun." So even if he falls into the ocean, he has had an astonishing experience.

To a Friend Whose Work Has Come to Triumph
Anne Sexton

Consider Icarus, pasting those sticky wings on,
testing that strange little tug at his shoulder blade,
and think of that first flawless moment over the lawn
of the labyrinth. Think of the difference it made!
There below are the trees, as awkward as camels;
and here are the shocked starlings pumping past
and think of innocent Icarus who is doing quite well:
larger than a sail, over the fog and the blast
of the plushy ocean, he goes. Admire his wings!
Feel the fire at his neck and see how casually
he glances up and is caught, wondrously tunneling ?
into that hot eye. Who cares that he fell back to the sea?
See him acclaiming the sun and come plunging down
while his sensible daddy goes straight into town.

Collaborating is a useful reading strategy. After reading and marking up the text, get together with others in your class to share ideas about the poem's meaning and talk out your questions. While you will not come to a full interpretation after this initial interaction, you can make some comments about first impressions. Note what the reader of the poem wrote in the margins.

Here is another poem by Anne Sexton—it is about a painting by Vincent van Gogh. Try your hand at annotating. Mark down all of your initial reactions. The purpose of annotating is to make your thinking visible on the page as you read.

The Starry Night
Anne Sexton

*That does not keep me from having a terrible need of—
shall I say the word—religion. Then I go out at night to
paint the stars.*
(Vincent van Gogh in a letter to his brother)

The town does not exist
except where one black-haired tree slips
up like a drowned woman into the hot sky.
The town is silent. The night boils with eleven stars.
Oh starry starry night! This is how
I want to die.

It moves. They are all alive.
Even the moon bulges in its orange irons
to push children, like a god, from its eye.
The old unseen serpent swallows up the stars.
Oh starry starry night! This is how
I want to die:

into that rushing beast of the night,
sucked up by that great dragon, to split
from my life with no flag,
no belly,
no cry.

Make a sketch of what you think van Gogh's painting looks like. Take your clues from the title and from the lines in the poem that refer to it.

12

●◆ Talk with a partner or in a group about Sexton's poem. Share ideas and questions from your annotations and your drawing. Then write a brief summary of the poem as you understand it so far.

Active readers engage in a dialogue with the author as they read. They interact with the work of literature by underlining, asking questions, drawing, and jotting down ideas.

Two Story Connections

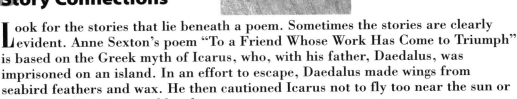

Look for the stories that lie beneath a poem. Sometimes the stories are clearly evident. Anne Sexton's poem "To a Friend Whose Work Has Come to Triumph" is based on the Greek myth of Icarus, who, with his father, Daedalus, was imprisoned on an island. In an effort to escape, Daedalus made wings from seabird feathers and wax. He then cautioned Icarus not to fly too near the sun or the wax in the wings would melt.

The story of Icarus is a myth that echoes human experiences, with numerous parallels in everyday life. You may remember the story of James Dean, the famous actor who died in a fiery car crash caused by his speeding in his fancy sports car. He became even more famous after death. Marilyn Monroe is another idol of Hollywood who lived recklessly and died young. Today she is adored by fans who are caught by the tragedy of a young life cut off prematurely.

What stories from your own experience does Icarus make you think of? Trace the threads that connect your stories with the myth of Icarus by creating a word cluster, drawing a picture, or writing a description.

Reread "The Starry Night." Imagine a scenario that might have given rise to this poem. Think of a time in your own life, for example, when some aspect of the sky or of nature led you to reflect on ideas.

●◆ Describe your scenario. Include the **setting** (time and place) and what happened. Then write about the ideas that you reflected on in this situation. You may write your response in two or three paragraphs or, if you feel poetic, **stanzas**.

14

Active readers look not only for the stories behind a work—such as myths or biographical information— but also for experiences in their own lives that parallel the stories in the work.

Three
Shifting Perspectives

One of the ways to read a piece of literature is to ask "what if" questions and to speculate about alternatives. For example, in focusing on the title of a work, you might consider how different titles would change the meaning for you. Asking "what if" will lead you back to "what is."

Speculate with a partner on how you might read "To a Friend Whose Work Has Come to Triumph":

- if the title were different. What other title would fit this poem? How would this different title affect its meaning for you? How many possibilities can you come up with for a title different from the one that Sexton chose?

- if Icarus were a story of a mother and a daughter. How would this change affect your understanding or your feelings about the poem?

- if you were a parent who had lost a child because of an accident.

"To a Friend Whose Work Has Come to Triumph" is a new slant on an old story. Literature is filled with stories and poems that have risen from shifts in perspective. The story of Icarus has been recast many times, in paintings as well as in poems.

Try your hand at recasting this story in another way. Some possibilities include: as a drawing; as a dialogue between two friends, one of whom wants to try something daring; or as a conversation between a parent and child. In the space below, sketch out your ideas as preparation. You may want to create a cluster or an outline.

15

●◆ Now recast the poem.

Shifting
perspectives in a
text will help you
develop insight into
the original work as
well as possibilities
for your own
writing.

Four
Language and Craft

Studying an author's use of language and craft provides another avenue of understanding. With poetry, form is so closely bound up with meaning that it needs to be explored. Some **verse forms**, such as **free verse**, are very loose. Others have rules that govern such matters as **line** length, **rhythm**, and **rhyme scheme**. Anne Sexton worked with very strict forms in many of her poems. "To a Friend Whose Work Has Come to Triumph," for example, is a Shakespearean **sonnet**.

Reread "The Starry Night" and review your annotations. In the chart below, jot down in the left column words and phrases you find interesting or provocative. In the right column, explain why you chose these words.

Words and phrases from the poem	Reasons for choosing them

17

Looking closely at language and form increases your ability to read sympathetically, almost as if you were reading as the writer would.

Five

Focus on the Writer

Reading one or two poems by an author gives you some insight into his or her work as a whole. The more you read a specific author, however, the better you will come to understand each piece. Knowing something of an author's life, culture, and the historical period in which he or she wrote can also extend your understanding of the author's work as a whole.

Anne Sexton's life has been the subject of intense scrutiny. She eloped at the age of nineteen and had two children before she even began to write seriously. She experienced strong emotional swings, and even serious breakdowns. When she was recovering from a mental breakdown, she experienced what she called "a rebirth at twenty-nine" and began writing poetry. Her first volume was titled *To Bedlam and Part Way Back*, clearly a personal history of her experiences. Sexton's poems are generally frank about her own life.

At the age of forty-six, Sexton committed suicide. Maxine Kumin, another poet—who had encouraged Sexton in her early days of writing—was a close friend and poetic confidante. After Sexton's death, Kumin wrote about their friendship. Here are a few extracts from Kumin's essay "A Friendship Remembered."

from **"A Friendship Remembered"** by Maxine Kumin

←—Response notes—→

18

As the world knows, we were intimate friends and professional allies. Early on in our friendship, indeed almost as soon as we began to share poems, we began to share them on the telephone. . . . It was her habit, when alone at night (and alone at night meant depressed always, sometimes anxious to the point of pain as well) to call on old friends. But that's a digression. What I wanted to say was I don't know what year, but fairly early on, we both installed second phone lines in our houses so that the rest of each of our families—the two husbands, the five children—could have equal access to a phone and we could talk privately for as long as we wanted. I confess we sometimes connected with a phone call and kept that line linked for hours at a stretch, interrupting poem-talk to stir the spaghetti sauce, switch the laundry, or try out a new image on the typewriter; we whistled into the receiver for each other when we were ready to resume. It worked wonders. . . .

Writing poems and bouncing them off each other by phone does develop the ear. You learn to hear line breaks, to pick up and be critical of unintended internal rhyme, or intended slant rhyme or whatever.

Now read "The Fury of Overshoes." Imagine that Sexton has just finished writing it and is reading it to you over the telephone. Make notes in the margin about what you want to say when she has finished reading.

The Fury of Overshoes
Anne Sexton

They sit in a row
outside the kindergarten,
black, red, brown, all
with those brass buckles.
Remember when you couldn't
buckle your own
overshoe
or tie your own
shoe
or cut your own meat
and the tears
running down like mud
because you fell off your
tricycle?
Remember, big fish,
when you couldn't swim
and simply slipped under
like a stone frog?
The world wasn't
yours.
It belonged to
the big people.
Under your bed
sat the wolf
and he made a shadow
when cars passed by
at night.
They made you give up
your nightlight
and your teddy
and your thumb.
Oh overshoes,
don't you
remember me,
pushing you up and down
in the winter snow?
Oh thumb,
I want a drink,
it is dark,
where are the big people,
when will I get there,
taking giant steps
all day,
each day
and thinking
nothing of it?

Response notes

19

You have just heard this poem for the first time. Look at your response notes and write the conversation that you might have with Sexton about the poem. It might begin like this:

Sexton: *Okay, what do you think?*

You: *I was so busy remembering what it was like to be a little kid, I've forgotten half of it.*

Sexton: *What parts made you remember?*

●◆ Now, write your own dialogue.

20

Fact Meets Fiction

From Colonial times onward, fiction describing our country's history has appeared as factual stories. Many early American novelists—James Fenimore Cooper is one example—encouraged readers to believe that their portrayals of events, people, or regions were true. It is often difficult to determine the fine line that separates fact and fiction. But, we can examine how writers use historical (and personal) experiences in their fiction and to what ends.

Some writers use history to give a veil of authenticity to a purely fictional work. Others use history to reimagine and reinterpret historical events. Still other writers have said that fiction helps them examine the interior lives of people who lived long ago. For example, Toni Morrison said that she wrote the novel *Beloved* as a way "to conjure up what was real" in the lives of those who were slaves. Whatever the purpose, it is helpful to remember that the story that gets written down is a product of a writer's mind. The story is one version of the many stories that could be told.

One

Historical Details in a Story

Some writers create historical situations in their stories. They use real places and recognizable events to make the world they create appear as if it were true. Charles Johnson's novel *Middle Passage* is the story of a fictional mutiny aboard a slave ship, the *Republic*, in 1830. The *Republic*'s mission is to transport the last survivors of a legendary tribe, the Allmuseri, to the New World. The story's narrator is Rutherford Calhoun, the ship's cook and a freed slave. Johnson created this fictional event to describe and recreate the reality of the Atlantic slave trade. The novel has been praised for the precision of its historical detail and won the 1990 National Book Award.

from *Middle Passage* by Charles Johnson

←—Response notes—→

Compared to other African tribes, the Allmuseri were the most popular servants. They brought twice the price of a Bantu or Kru. According to legend, Allmuseri elders took twig brooms with them everywhere, sweeping the ground so as not to inadvertently step on creatures too small to see. Eating no meat, they were easy to feed. Disliking property, they were simple to clothe. Able to heal themselves, they required no medication. They seldom fought. They could not steal. They fell *sick*, it was said, if they wronged anyone. As I live, they so shamed me I wanted their ageless culture to be my own, if in fact Ngonyama spoke truly. But who was I fooling? While Rutherford Calhoun might envy certain features of Allmuseri folkways, he could never claim something he had no hand in creating. I respected them too much to insult them this way—particularly one woman and her eight-year-old daughter, Baleka, who'd caught a biscuit I tossed her one day when talking to Meadows. Her mother snatched it away. She studied it like a woman inspecting melons at a public market, her face growing sharp. She smelled it, she tasted it with a tiny nibble, and spat it out the side of her mouth into the sea. Presently, she stumped across the deck and dropped it back onto my lap. Sliding up behind her, half hidden behind Mama's legs, Baleka stuck out her hand. Her eyes burned a hole in my forehead. Her mother's finger wagged in my face, and in the little of their language I knew she sniffed that her baby deserved far better than one moldy biscuit. I could only agree. To square things, that night I shared my powdered beef, mustard, and tea with Baleka: a major mistake. Her expectation, and that of Mama, for sharing my *every* pan of food became an unspoken contract no less binding between us than a handshake. By and by, we were inseparable. This was how Mama wanted it, having decided her child's survival might depend on staying close to the one crew member who looked most African, asking me to decipher the strange behavior of the whites and intercede on their behalf. Thus, the child stayed at my heels as I spun rope and, when I was on larboard watch by the taffrail, leaned against my legs, looking back sadly toward Senegambia.

Thus we were at five bells in the forenoon of June 11.

•✦ What details does Johnson use that seem factual? How do the details lend believability to the episode?

•✦ Explain how Johnson uses details to create a dramatic effect out of what might otherwise be the "dull facts" of history. Discuss whether or not you find Johnson's portrayal effective and explain why or why not.

Writers use historical details and situations in their fictional works to give an air of believability, to heighten the reality of a situation, and to create a sense of drama.

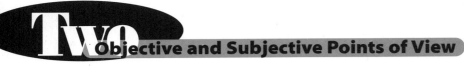

Two
Objective and Subjective Points of View

Through most of *Moby Dick*, Herman Melville tells the story through the minds of the narrator or characters—that is, from a **subjective point of view**. The subjective point of view is an interpretation of the facts and often an emotional reaction to them. However, interspersed throughout the novel are lengthy passages about whales and the profession of whaling. His intent was to help the reader understand the facts of whaling. These digressions are written from the **objective point of view**.

Writers often blend the objective and subjective to further the purposes of their books. N. Scott Momaday's *The Way to Rainy Mountain* combines the two points of view in a retelling of the history and traditions of the Kiowa, a tribe of Native Americans that was forced to move from the northern Plains to Oklahoma. His purpose is to illustrate the complex tribal history.

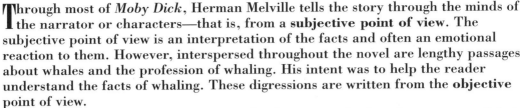

from ***The Way to Rainy Mountain*** by N. Scott Momaday

← *Response notes* →

The journey began one day long ago on the edge of the northern Plains. It was carried on over a course of many generations and many hundreds of miles. In the end there were many things to remember, to dwell upon and talk about.

"You know, everything had to begin. . . ." For the Kiowas the beginning was a struggle for existence in the bleak northern mountains. It was there, they say, that they entered the world through a hollow log. The end, too, was a struggle, and it was lost. The young Plains culture of the Kiowas withered and died like grass that is burned in the prairie wind. There came a day like destiny; in every direction, as far as the eye could see, carrion lay out in the land. The buffalo was the animal representation of the sun, the essential and sacrificial victim of the Sun Dance. When the wild herds were destroyed, so too was the will of the Kiowa people; there was nothing to sustain them in spirit. But these are idle recollections, the mean and ordinary agonies of human history. The interim was a time of great adventure and nobility and fulfillment.

Tai-me came to the Kiowas in a vision born of suffering and despair. "Take me with you," Tai-me said, "and I will give you whatever you want." And it was so. The great adventure of the Kiowas was a going forth into the heart of the continent. They began a long migration from the headwaters of the Yellowstone River eastward to the Black Hills and south to the Wichita Mountains. Along the way they acquired horses, the religion of the Plains, a love and possession of the open land. Their nomadic soul was set free. In alliance with the Comanches they held dominion in the southern Plains for a hundred years. In the course of that long migration they had come of age as a people. They had conceived a good idea of themselves; they had dared to imagine and determine who they were.

In one sense, then, the way to Rainy Mountain is preeminently the history of an idea, man's idea of himself, and it has old and essential being in language. The verbal tradition by which it has been preserved

from *The Way to Rainy Mountain* by N. Scott Momaday

← Response notes →

has suffered a deterioration in time. What remains is fragmentary: mythology, legend, lore, and hearsay—and of course the idea itself, as crucial and complete as it ever was. That is the miracle.

The journey herein recalled continues to be made anew each time the miracle comes to mind, for that is peculiarly the right and responsibility of the imagination. It is a whole journey, intricate with motion and meaning; and it is made with the whole memory, that experience of the mind which is legendary as well as historical, personal as well as cultural. And the journey is an evocation of three things in particular: a landscape that is incomparable, a time that is gone forever, and the human spirit, which endures. The imaginative experience and the historical express equally the traditions of man's reality. Finally, then, the journey recalled is among other things the revelation of one way in which these traditions are conceived, developed, and interfused in the human mind. There are on the way to Rainy Mountain many landmarks, many journeys in the one. From the beginning the migration of the Kiowas was an expression of the human spirit, and that expression is most truly made in terms of wonder and delight: "There were many people, and oh, it was beautiful. That was the beginning of the Sun Dance. It was all for Tai-me, you know, and it was a long time ago."

List objective and subjective details describing the Kiowas' journey on the chart below. Some examples are provided.

Objective	Subjective
several generations involved	importance of remembering
migrate hundreds of miles	

Compare your chart with that of a partner. Discuss what you learned from the objective and from the subjective details.

An objective point of view provides readers with factual information. The subjective point of view gives information about how events have been interpreted by the author, narrator, or characters.

Three
Storytelling in Multiple Voices

There are many versions of any story. The challenge for the writer is to decide how to structure the telling and how to distinguish one version from another. In *The Way to Rainy Mountain*, Momaday created a structure that allowed him to use multiple storytelling voices and create almost simultaneous tellings.

<— Response notes —>

from **The Way to Rainy Mountain** by N. Scott Momaday

Long ago there were bad times. The Kiowas were hungry and there was no food. There was a man who heard his children cry from hunger, and he went out to look for food. He walked four days and became very weak. On the fourth day he came to a great canyon. Suddenly there was thunder and lightning. A voice spoke to him and said, "Why are you following me? What do you want?" The man was afraid. The thing standing before him had the feet of a deer, and its body was covered with feathers. The man answered that the Kiowas were hungry. "Take me with you," the voice said, "and I will give you whatever you want." From that day Tai-me has belonged to the Kiowas.

The great central figure of the kado, *or Sun Dance, ceremony is the Tai-me. This is a small image, less than 2 feet in length, representing a human figure dressed in a robe of white feathers, with a headdress consisting of a single upright feather and pendants of ermine skin, with numerous strands of blue beads around its neck, and painted upon the face, breast, and back with designs symbolic of the sun and moon. The image itself is of dark-green stone, in form rudely resembling a human head and bust, probably shaped by art like the stone fetishes of the Pueblo tribes. It is preserved in a rawhide box in charge of the hereditary keeper, and is never under any circumstances exposed to view except at the annual Sun Dance, when it is fastened to a short upright stick planted within the medicine lodge, near the western side. It was last exposed in 1888.*
  —Mooney

Once I went with my father and grandmother to see the Tai-me bundle. It was suspended by means of a strip of ticking from the fork of a small ceremonial tree. I made an offering of bright red cloth, and my grandmother prayed aloud. It seemed a long time that we were there. I had never come into the presence of Tai-me before—nor have I since. There was a great holiness all about in the room, as if an old person had died there or a child had been born.

●◆ Write responses to the following questions:

1. Describe the storyteller in each paragraph. What does each contribute to your understanding of the Tai-me?

2. Which of the accounts is most vivid to you and why?

3. What information does each storyteller give that helps you understand the other accounts? Include examples to support your explanation.

Writers sometimes use multiple narrators to try to present some of the perspectives on a story. Readers need to identify who is telling the story and what each contributes to the larger idea.

Four Fictionalizing Personal Experience

Writers often draw on their personal experience. For example, Julia Alvarez's novel *How the García Girls Lost Their Accents*, tells the story of the four García sisters—Carla, Sandra, Yolanda, and Sofía—and their arrival in New York City in 1960. Alvarez herself immigrated to New York City from the Dominican Republic in 1960. In the following excerpt from one of the novel's interconnected stories below, you can get a sense of how Alvarez's own experiences helped her portray the fictional experience.

"Snow" from ***How the García Girls Lost Their Accents*** by Julia Alvarez

← Response notes →

Yolanda

Our first year in New York we rented a small apartment with a Catholic school nearby, taught by the Sisters of Charity, hefty women in long black gowns and bonnets that made them look peculiar, like dolls in mourning. I liked them a lot, especially my grandmotherly fourth grade teacher, Sister Zoe. I had a lovely name, she said, and she had me teach the whole class how to pronounce it. *Yo-lan-da*. As the only immigrant in my class, I was put in a special seat in the first row by the window, apart from the other children so that Sister Zoe could tutor me without disturbing them. Slowly, she enunciated the new words I was to repeat: *laundromat, corn flakes, subway, snow*.

Soon I picked up enough English to understand holocaust was in the air. Sister Zoe explained to a wide-eyed classroom what was happening in Cuba. Russian missiles were being assembled, trained supposedly on New York City. President Kennedy, looking worried too, was on the television at home, explaining we might have to go to war against the Communists. At school, we had air-raid drills: an ominous bell would go off and we'd file into the hall, fall to the floor, cover our heads with our coats, and imagine our hair falling out, the bones in our arms going soft. At home, Mami and my sisters and I said a rosary for world peace. I heard new vocabulary: *nuclear bomb, radioactive fallout, bomb shelter*. Sister Zoe explained how it would happen. She drew a picture of a mushroom on the blackboard and dotted a flurry of chalkmarks for the dusty fallout that would kill us all.

The months grew cold, November, December. It was dark when I got up in the morning, frosty when I followed my breath to school. One morning as I sat at my desk daydreaming out the window, I saw dots in the air like the ones Sister Zoe had drawn—random at first, then lots and lots. I shrieked, "Bomb! Bomb!" Sister Zoe jerked around, her full black skirt ballooning as she hurried to my side. A few girls began to cry.

But then Sister Zoe's shocked look faded. "Why, Yolanda dear, that's snow!" She laughed. "Snow."

"Snow," I repeated. I looked out the window warily. All my life I had heard about the white crystals that fell out of American skies in the winter. From my desk I watched the fine powder dust the sidewalk and parked cars below. Each flake was different, Sister Zoe had said, like a person, irreplaceable and beautiful.

28

●◆ Alvarez has said that she wanted through her fiction to bring her readers some acquaintance with worlds other than the ones they know. How successfully does Alvarez acquaint you with a world other than the one you know? Use details from "Snow" to support your opinion.

....

....

....

....

....

....

....

....

....

....

....

●◆ Now write a paragraph about a memorable moment in your life.

....

....

....

....

....

....

....

....

....

....

●◆Rewrite your paragraph as a fictionalized version of the experience. In this paragraph, create a character to narrate the story for you.

Writers often fictionalize their experiences to enhance the dramatic effect.

Read both of your paragraphs to a partner. Discuss similarities and differences in the emphasis in each.

Five Details Tell the Story

Tim O'Brien fought in the Vietnam War, earning a Purple Heart during his two-year tour of duty. O'Brien wrote about his experiences in several fictional episodes and explained his purpose for inventing rather than recording what is true: "It's kind of a semantic game: lying versus truth-telling. . . . One doesn't lie for the sake of lying; one does not invent merely for the sake of inventing. One does it for a particular purpose and that purpose always is to arrive at some kind of spiritual truth that one can't discover simply by recording the world-as-it-is. We're inventing and using imagination for sublime reasons—to get at the essence of things, not merely the surface."

In the excerpt below, a soldier, Mitchell Sanders, tells the story about a six-man patrol that gets spooked while waiting in the jungle for a week. They begin to hear many different kinds of music and eventually have the whole area bombed. The next morning, Sanders reflects on the "truth" of the story he told.

from "How to Tell a True War Story" from ***The Things They Carried***
by Tim O'Brien

You can tell a true war story by the way it never seems to end. Not then, not ever. Not when Mitchell Sanders stood up and moved off into the dark.

It all happened.

Even now, at this instant, I remember that yo-yo. In a way, I suppose, you had to be there, you had to hear it, but I could tell how desperately Sanders wanted me to believe him, his frustration at not quite getting the details right, not quite pinning down the final and definitive truth.

And I remember sitting at my foxhole that night, watching the shadows of Quang Ngai, thinking about the coming day and how we would cross the river and march west into the mountains, all the ways I might die, all the things I did not understand.

Late in the night Mitchell Sanders touched my shoulder.

"Just came to me," he whispered. "The moral, I mean. Nobody listens. Nobody hears nothin'. Like that fatass colonel. The politicians, all the civilian types. Your girlfriend. My girlfriend. Everybody's sweet little virgin girlfriend. What they need is to go out on LP. The vapors, man. Trees and rocks—you got to *listen* to your enemy."

And then again, in the morning, Sanders came up to me. The platoon was preparing to move out, checking weapons, going through all the little rituals that preceded a day's march. Already the lead squad had crossed the river and was filing off toward the west.

"I got a confession to make," Sanders said. "Last night, man, I had to make up a few things."

"I know that."

"The glee club. There wasn't any glee club."

"Right."

"No opera."

"Forget it, I understand."

← *Response notes* →

31

from "How to Tell a True War Story" from ***The Things They Carried***
by Tim O'Brien

"Yeah, but listen, it's still true. Those six guys, they heard wicked sounds out there. They heard sound you just plain won't believe."

Sanders pulled on his rucksack, closed his eyes for a moment, then almost smiled at me. I knew what was coming.

"All right," I said, "what's the moral?"

"Forget it."

"No, go ahead."

For a long while he was quiet, looking away, and the silence kept stretching out until it was almost embarrassing. Then he shrugged and gave me a stare that lasted all day.

"Hear that quiet, man?" he said. "That quiet—just listen. There's your moral."

In a true war story, if there's a moral at all, it's like the thread that makes the cloth. You can't tease it out. You can't extract the meaning without unraveling the deeper meaning. And in the end, really, there's nothing much to say about a true war story, except maybe "Oh."

True war stories do not generalize. They do not indulge in abstraction or analysis.

For example: War is hell. As a moral declaration the old truism seems perfectly true, and yet because it abstracts, because it generalizes, I can't believe it with my stomach. Nothing turns inside.

It comes down to gut instinct. A true war story, if truly told, makes the stomach believe.

●✦ What do you think O'Brien means by the statement: "True war stories do not generalize. They do not indulge in abstraction or analysis"? What does this mean? Do you agree or disagree with the idea that abstraction cannot make "the stomach believe"?

The details of a story can sometimes be far more important to the reader than any abstractions or generalizations that are made.

The Nonfiction Novel

Literature is often classified into genres—categories that separate poems from plays, short stories, novels, essays, and so on. Each genre uses distinct forms and techniques that distinguish one from another. However, classification is never simple. Writers have borrowed characteristics of one genre to use in another, creating new types of literature. For example, during the past twenty years, a new genre has developed from the combination of the narrative techniques of fiction with the facts of journalistic reporting. Journalists, travel writers, biographers, and historians seldom worried about storytelling, focusing instead on description and facts. However, in the 1960s writers began combining journalistic reporting with the literary techniques used in the novel. What resulted were vivid portrayals of real events with the immediacy and emotional power of a novel.

In mid-August of 1949, Norman Maclean saw the Mann Gulch forest fire burning in Montana. About two weeks earlier, a crew of fifteen Smokejumpers from the United States Forest Service's airborne firefighters had entered Montana's remote wilderness to fight the fire. Less than two hours later, all but three of them were dead. Exactly what happened is not known, but Maclean spent the last fourteen years of his life piecing the story together as best he could. From what he learned, Maclean assembled a story of the tragedy in *Young Men and Fire*.

from *Young Men and Fire* by Norman Maclean

←—Response notes—→

When the smoke started mixing at night with my dreams, I locked my cabin and drove the 150 miles to Wolf Creek and picked up my brother-in-law, who had fought a few days on the Mann Gulch fire as a volunteer. He and I borrowed a Dodge Power Wagon from the Oxbow Ranch, because we knew it would be tough going ahead. Then we drove up the dirt road on the east side of the Missouri until we came to the Gates of the Mountains and to Willow Creek, the creek north of Mann Gulch where the fire was finally stopped on its downriver side. The road went up the creek for a way and then dead-ended, and it and the creek had been used by the crew—on the whole, successfully—as fire-lines. Only occasionally had the fire jumped both of them, and where it had the crew quickly controlled it again. By the time we reached the fire the crew had put it out for several hundred yards back of the road or creek, sawing down the still-burning trees and either burying them with dirt or pouring water on them when they were near the creek. Since there was no danger of the fire jumping the lines again, the crew had moved on, leaving the fire to burn itself harmlessly in its interior.

It was a world of still-warm ashes that had incubated once-hot poles.

Maclean returns years later to continue his research. He began to collect eyewitness accounts, research smokejumping and other firefighting techniques, and study records of subsequent fires in the area. A good researcher must be a good observer and questioner and have the instinct to distinguish what is important. As you read the following scene from *Young Men and Fire*, consider what information Maclean must have learned in order to write the passage.

The fire was located in the "Gates of the Mountains" wild area (roadless area) just east of the Missouri River, some twenty miles north of Helena . . . at a point near the top of the ridge between Mann and Meriwether gulches. The general area is steep and jagged on the Meriwether side and is said to be one of the roughest areas east of the Continental Divide.

from the official *Report of Board of Review*, Mann Gulch fire
Helena National Forest, August 5, 1949

from *Young Men and Fire* by Norman Maclean

← Response notes →

Mann Gulch is a dry gulch two and a half miles long that runs into the lower end of the spectacular stretch of the Missouri River called the Gates of the Mountains by the first white man who entered them, Captain Meriwether Lewis, when on July 19, 1805, he camped his party at the mouth of the gulch now bearing his first name. Immediately downriver from Meriwether Canyon is Mann Gulch, where the fire started near the top of the ridge between the two gulches, and almost immediately downriver from these two gulches the Gates open to the plains.

"From the singular appearance of this place I called it the gates of the rocky mountains," Captain Lewis said in his journals. Its singular appearance makes it a fitting backdrop for early and everlasting drama in which nature plays the leading role. If you are coming upstream from yellow flat plains, as Captain Lewis and Captain Clark had been for over a year, you can observe even at a great distance how there is something about mountains that hates to be plains. Far, far ahead are the mountains black with the haze that makes mountains look from the plains as if they were clouds of smoke from a great forest fire. As they and you come closer, the haze of the mountains breaks apart and reluctantly allows the yellow plains a final appearance. This is literally the way it was in Mann Gulch before the fire burned it out in a matter of minutes. It was the place in the Gates where the struggle between mountains and plains came face to face—below Mann Gulch belongs to the plains, upriver to the mountains and timber. Mann Gulch itself where the grave markers are was yellow with tall grass. The differences are not only scenic— there are differences between the behavior of grass and timber fires, and the differences can be tragic if firefighters don't know them.

●◆ Read the passage again, and try to reconstruct the information Maclean needed to learn about Mann Gulch and the fire to write this paragraph. Write about how Maclean adds dramatic effect and immediacy to the details.

A good researcher presents the key facts. A good storyteller then uses the techniques of fiction to help add immediacy and dramatic effect to real-life situations.

35

Two

Cinematic Scenes

Maclean spent years gathering information and visiting Mann Gulch. He had to determine how to organize his research. Maclean wrote the various stories and information he gathered as a series of cinematic scenes ranging in length from one paragraph to several pages. Notice how Maclean helps you visualize the Gulch in the following scene.

from ***Young Men and Fire*** by Norman Maclean

← Response notes →

Jansson walked up the bottom of Mann Gulch for almost half a mile, noting that the fire was picking up momentum and still throwing smoke over his head to the north side of the gulch where farther up Dodge had rejoined his crew and was now leading them toward the river. Then right behind Jansson at the bottom of the gulch a spot fire flowered. Then several more flowered just below the main fire. Then a few tossed themselves as bouquets across the gulch, grew rapidly into each other's flames, and became a garden of wildfire.

What the ranger was about to see was the beginning of the blowup. Seemingly without relation to reality or to the workings of the imagination, the flowers that had grown into a garden distended themselves into an enormous light bulb and a great mixed metaphor. Flowers and light bulbs don't seem to mix, but the light bulb of the mind strung itself inside with filaments of flame and flowers, bloated and rounded itself at its top with gases, then swirled upgulch to meet the Smokejumpers trying to escape downgulch. In a few minutes they met. Then only a few minutes later the blowup passed out of the gulch, blew its fuse, and left a world that is still burned out.

●◆ Sketch two scenes of the blowup. Sketching will help you organize the details into actual images. Do not worry about your artistic ability.

Authors need to organize their information with concrete descriptions to help the reader see the scene.

Share your drawings with others and discuss how each of you visualized the blowup.

Three
Horizontal and Vertical Tellings

Truman Capote, author of the nonfiction novel *In Cold Blood*, wrote that: "Journalism always moves along on a horizontal plane, telling a story, moves vertically, taking you deeper and deeper into character and events." A horizontal telling moves through a series of events. The vertical telling lingers over people's interior lives and the meaning of events, providing details that dwell on how particular people acted, reacted, and explained events. In the following scene, notice the horizontal and vertical telling in Maclean's description of the blowout.

from *Young Men and Fire* by Norman Maclean

Although Jansson thought he had put out of mind the possibility that the jumpers or anything human besides himself could be in Mann Gulch, he began to hear metallic noises that sounded like men working. That's the sound of flames heard by those alive after the flames go by. It is the thinking of those living who think they can hear dead men still at work.

Even with the flames closing in, Jansson had to follow the sounds in his head another eighth of a mile upgulch until any possibility that men were working in Mann Gulch had been obliterated. While he walked that eighth of a mile, the crown fire on the north-facing slope behind him had burned to the bottom of the gulch and the spot fires that had jumped to the opposite slope had converged behind him into one fire coming upgulch at him.

This fire front on the south-facing slope was in a few minutes to become the blaze only seventy-five yards behind the Smokejumpers after they dumped their heavy tools to run faster, and the crown fire which Jansson saw moving into the bottom of the gulch was to become the roar the Smokejumpers heard below them at almost the same time. At almost the same time everything was closing in on them and Jansson.

At 5:30 Jansson turned back and started to get out of there quick but still walking. Then the fire began to whirl continuously. When a streamer from it swept by, he realized after a couple of whiffs that the whirl could "cook out his lungs." He began to run. Now, he says, the whirl "was practically upright. My position was in the vortex, which was rapidly narrowing. I held my breath as I crossed the wall. There was no flame, just superheated air and gases and a lot of reflected heat from the crown fire. I conked out from a lack of oxygen, fell on my left elbow, causing a bursitus which later caused my arm to swell."

When he came to, "the black creep of the fire" was only a few feet behind him. He had fallen victim for a few seconds to the two major enemies that threaten fighters of big fires—toxic gases, especially carbon monoxide, and lack of oxygen from overexertion and from hot air burning out the oxygen.

When he finally reached the boat, at 5:41, he placed himself in the bow next to Mrs. Padbury and watched the whirl for a few minutes. He thought again about the sound of men working that he imagined he had heard and again put it out of mind. Then he smelled his own vomit, apologized to Mrs. Padbury, and moved off to the side.

At the Board of Review, he was asked this question, to which he

←— *Response notes* —→

37

← Response notes →

gave a short answer:

GUSTAFSON: In looking back up Mann Gulch draw . . . what was the picture as to the fire at that time?

JANSSON: A blowup.

Before the Padbury boat reached Meriwether Landing, superintendent Moir was in midriver in a speedboat preparing to go downstream. When the two boats met, Jansson transferred to the speedboat, and they landed where they could climb to an observation point giving them a complete view of Mann Gulch. Jansson says, "At that time it was apparent that all of Mann Gulch had burned out, but it appeared that the big blowup in Mann Gulch was over."

"At that time" can only be estimated, but it was shortly after six o'clock. When all is said and done, we still accept the hands of Jim Harrison's watch, which were melted permanently at about four minutes to six, as marking approximately the time that the fire was catching up to the crew.

About twenty minutes had passed between the time that Jansson left the mouth of Mann Gulch and the time he turned to view the whole of it. Near at hand, trees still exploded from the heat of their own resin, at a distance vast sounds were being converted into silent lights and the lights were being turned off, and nowhere were there any longer noises as of men working.

38

Reconstruct this scene into a timeline of events (the horizontal telling). Start by listing six to eight events on the timeline.

Jansson hears metallic noises | Jansson walks an eighth of a mile | **3** | **4** | **5** | **6** | **7** | **8**

●◆ Now, point out places where Maclean lingers over details (the vertical telling) that elaborate on what happens. In the log below, list the details (vertical telling) that explain the events listed on your timeline.

Event	Vertical Telling
1.	thinks men are working; actually it's the sound of flames
2.	
3.	
4.	
5.	
6.	
7.	
8.	

Horizontal description provides information about what happened. Vertical description helps reveal the significance of the events and details.

Four Digressions

Sebastian Junger's book *The Perfect Storm* documents the sinking of the fishing boat the *Andrea Gail* and the drowning of its six crew members off the coast of Nova Scotia in October 1991. Junger depicts the world of the fishermen, describes the fury of the storm, and recounts other stories of ship disasters. Junger was inspired to research this story from a newspaper article: "My own experience in the storm was limited to standing on Gloucester's Back Short watching thirty-foot swells advance on Cape Ann, but that was all it took. The next day I read in the paper that a Gloucester boat was feared lost at sea, and I clipped the article and stuck it in a drawer. Without even knowing it, I had begun to write *The Perfect Storm*." Junger uses the technique of **digression**—that is, to turn away from the main story (of the violent storm and the ship going down) to give related information. He describes the history of the fishing industry, the science of storms, and provides candid accounts of other people whose lives the storm touched.

from *The Perfect Storm* by Sebastian Junger

←—Response notes—→

Everyone on a sinking boat reacts differently. A man on one Gloucester boat just curled up and started to cry while his shipmates worked untethered on deck. The *Andrea Gail* crew, all experienced fishermen, are probably trying to shrug it off as just another storm—they've been through this before, they'll go through it again, and at least they're not puking. Billy's undoubtedly working too hard at the helm to give drowning much thought. Ernie Hazard claims it was the last thing on his mind. "There was no conversation, just real business-like," he says of going down off Georges Bank. "You know, 'Let's just get this thing done.' Never any overwhelming sense of danger. We were just very, very busy."

Be that as it may, certain realities still must come crashing in. At some point Tyne, Shatford, Sullivan, Moran, Murphy, and Pierre must realize there's no way off this boat. They could trigger the EPIRB, but a night rescue in these conditions would be virtually impossible. They could deploy the life raft, but they probably wouldn't survive the huge seas. If the boat goes down, they go down with it, and no one on earth can do anything about it. Their lives are utterly and completely in their own hands.

That fact must settle into Bobby Shatford's stomach like a bad meal. It was he, after all, who had those terrible misgivings the day they left. That last afternoon on the dock he came within a hair's breadth of saying no—just telling Chris to start up the car and drive. They could have gone back to her place, or up the coast, or anywhere at all. It wouldn't have mattered; he wouldn't be in this storm right now, and neither would the rest of them. It would have taken Billy at least a day to replace him, and right now they'd still be east with the rest of the fleet.

The previous spring Bobby and Chris rented a movie called *The Fighting Sullivans*, about five brothers who died on a U.S. Navy boat during World War Two. It was Ethel's favorite movie. Sitting there with Chris, watching the movie, and thinking about his brothers, Bobby started to cry. He was not a man who cried easily and Chris

39

from ***The Perfect Storm*** by Sebastian Junger

←—Response notes—→

was unsure what to do. Should she say something? Pretend not to notice? Turn off the T.V.? Finally, Bobby said that he was upset by the idea of all his brothers fishing, and that if anything happened to *him*, he wanted to be buried at sea. Chris said that nothing was going to happen to him, but he insisted. Just bury me at sea, he said. Promise me that.

And now here he is, getting buried at sea. The conditions have degenerated from bad to unspeakable, Beaufort Force 10 or 11. The British *Manual of Seamanship* describes a Force 10 gale as: "Foam is in great patches and is blown in dense white streaks along the direction of the wind. The rolling of the sea becomes heavy and shock-like." Force 11 is even worse: "Exceptionally high waves, small or medium-sized ships might be lost from view behind them. The sea is completely covered with long patches of white foam." Hurricane Grace is still working her way north, and when she collides with the Sable Island storm—probably in a day or so—conditions will get even more severe, maybe as high as Force 12. Very few boats that size can withstand a Force 12 gale.

Highlight the sections that you think represent digressions from the main story. A digression will be information that does not directly document the effect of Hurricane Grace on the *Andrea Gail* and the resulting deaths of the crew. Next to your markings, indicate what the digression adds to the story—background information, narrative or dramatic effect, and examples of similar incidents.

●◆ Write an explanation that 1) summarizes what two of the digressions are about, 2) describes their purpose in the story, and 3) explains the effect of each one.

....

....

....

....

....

....

....

....

Writers use digressions to provide readers with additional insight and meaning that cannot be revealed through the story or plot line.

Five
Recreating Experience

Junger also recreated the experience of the last days, hours, and minutes of the six men who died at sea. He wanted to write a factual book that would be respectable journalism. But, he also wanted to create a compelling narrative that would bring the danger and last moments vividly to life. As he explained, "Recreating the last days of six men who disappeared at sea presented some obvious problems for me. . . . If I didn't know exactly what happened aboard the doomed boat, for example, I would interview people who had been through similar situations, and survived. Their experiences, I felt, would provide a fairly good description of what the six men on the *Andrea Gail* had gone through, and said, and perhaps even felt." As Junger suggests, recreating the experience of real rather than fictional people has its challenges. In what follows, you will read his attempt to show the crew's final moments.

from *The Perfect Storm* by Sebastian Junger

←— *Response notes* —→

When a boat floods, the first thing that happens is that her electrical system shorts out. The lights go off, and for a few moments the only illumination is the frenetic blue of sparks arcing down into the water. It's said that people in extreme situations perceive things in distorted, almost surreal ways, and when the wires start to crackle and burn, perhaps one of the crew thinks of fireworks—of the last Fourth of July, walking around Gloucester with his girlfriend and watching colors blossom over the inner harbor. There'd be tourists shuffling down Rogers Street and fishermen hooting from bars and the smell of gunpowder and fried clams drifting through town. He'd have his whole life ahead of him, that July evening; he'd have every choice in the world.

And he wound up swordfishing. He wound up, by one route or another, on this trip, in this storm, with this boat filling up with water and one or two minutes left to live. There's no going back now, no rescue helicopter that could possibly save him. All that's left is to hope it's over fast.

When the water first hits the trapped men, it's cold but not paralyzing, around 52 degrees. A man can survive up to four hours in that temperature if something holds him up. If the boat rolls or flips over, the men in the wheelhouse are the first to drown. . . . they inhale and that's it. After that the water rises up the companionway, flooding the galley and berths, and then starts up the inverted engine room hatch. It may well be pouring in the aft door and the fish hatch, too, if either failed during the sinking. If the boat is hull-up and there are men in the engine room, they are the last to die. They're in absolute darkness, under a landslide of tools and gear, the water rising up the companionway and the roar of the waves probably very muted through the hull. If the water takes long enough, they might attempt to escape on a lungful of air—down the companionway, along the hall through the aft door and out from under the boat—but they don't make it. It's too far, they die trying. Or the water comes up so

41

hard and fast that they can't even think. They're up to their waists and then their chests and then their chins and then there's no air at all. Just what's in their lungs, a minute's worth or so.

To recreate experience, a writer needs to make conjectures. A conjecture—a surmise or guess—takes various forms in writing. Junger writes: "It's said," "perhaps one of the crew thinks," "If the boat. . . ." In each case, he reminds his readers that he is making guesses about what the crew experienced during their final moments. Highlight places in the text where you think Junger reminds you that he is surmising as he recreates the experience.

●◆ What do you think of the nonfiction novel as a genre? Do you think it is a valid genre? What are its strengths? weaknesses? Why do you think a novelist or journalist would try this hybrid genre?

....
....
....

....
....
....
....
....
....
....
....
....
....
....

Readers need to be aware of the differences between fact and conjecture when they interpret a nonfiction story.

Seeing the Landscape

What do you do when you read? Do you look at each word, trying to make sense of how they all go together? Do you create mental movies to get a complete picture of the setting and characters?

Authors help by providing various kinds of details to trigger concrete images in the reader's mind. Sensory details appeal to the senses, especially sight, sound, smell, and touch. Emotional details fill out the picture with the author's feelings and memories.

Many authors use the setting to reveal characteristics of a place or a person. Landscapes can also reflect personal insights and values. Seeing the landscape means using the author's words to construct a complete picture in your mind. The more fully you can envision the setting and characters, the better you will understand what you read. Being aware of how the author's personal view affects the description will also help you read critically. Some readers skip over "the long, descriptive parts." Active readers know how important it is to pay attention to every detail.

One A Landscape of Beauty and Fear

No one was more involved in his stories than journalist Ernie Pyle. In the late 1930s and early 1940s, he traveled across the country, writing a daily newspaper column about people and places. Editor David Nichols explained that Pyle wanted Americans to know about all parts of the country, not just the big cities: "At great cost to himself, Pyle worked hard arguing for the specificity of person and place as an important part of our American past and present."

"Ahead of the Night" by Ernie Pyle

←— Response notes —→

Falling snow is a beautiful thing almost anywhere. But when snow comes falling on a dark day down into the deep and narrow valleys of the Cumberland Mountains—as it does frequently and with an awful immensity—there is about it not only beauty but a strange fearfulness.

Somehow you feel that snow and low clouds and mountains and darkness are all coming down upon you, and this is the end of everything, and there will never be sunlight or another day.

•

The Cumberland Mountains start in central Tennessee and run northeastward up through the corner of Kentucky and on into Virginia. In a car you can make a circle and touch all three states in one afternoon and never be out of the Cumberlands.

They are beautiful, even in the leaflessness of winter. They are not immense, like the Rockies; nor regimented in strips, like the Blue Ridge; nor equipped with vast vistas, like the San Jacinto in California. They are indeed none of these, but a terrific serration, like measles.

•

The valleys are narrow, very seldom more than a city block wide at the bottom. The hills rise sharply on either side. They are covered with trees, and great ledges of rock strata protrude.

The valleys are crooked. You can't see far in the bottom of a Cumberland valley, for it always makes a turn just a little way ahead. Usually there is a stream in the valley, and the road winds along the stream; you see hillside corn patches, and log cabins and old barns, and now and then you pass through a village.

Always in the Cumberlands you must raise your head to see the sky, for all around, everywhere, are peaks. But in snowtime the peaks are missing. They vanish in gray mist that reaches down their sides and propels itself across the valleys to the other peaks, making a ceiling that closes you in.

•

44

"Ahead of the Night" by Ernie Pyle

The snow starts in Virginia. For a few minutes it falls timidly, feeling its way. The big wet flakes float down slowly, and they stand out sharply against the dark background of forested hillside.

Then it becomes a cold encompassing flood. Where there were two flakes, now there are thousands. Half the atmosphere must be snow. The flakes change direction, from vertical to horizontal, and come head-on like rushing atoms.

Swiftly as a tropical dusk, the light goes out of the valleys. Twilight comes in midafternoon. Mountain cabins are dim things through a downward-sliding screen. Trees and hillsides and sheds and fences accumulate a covering of gray. And you feel the darkness, as surely as you feel the cold.

And you know the foreboding, the sense of an impending end to all things. Through your mind run, over and over, the dark lines: "The shades of night were falling fast, when through an Alpine village passed, a youth . . ."

Men chop wood in their barnyards, frantically, as though stopping a leak in a dike. Horses stand in fence corners, tails to the snow, but ears alert, as if listening for doom around the bend. Workmen speed homeward, before it is too late. Life rushes to get in ahead of the night. Soon there is no movement in the valley— only the snow, and lonesomeness, and a feeling of being all alone in a land of strange forces, and an intuition that something will happen.

You don't imagine some specific things that might happen, nothing so material as a wreck or a murder, but something unreal and vaguely sinister. You want to speed, faster and faster.

•

That's what a blizzard in a Cumberland mountain valley does to a tenderfoot. The people there, I suppose, don't feel that way about it at all.

And in my own case, of course, nothing happened. I am here tonight in the room of a little inn, in a mountain village, and I feel so superior and safe. The radiator sizzles and the electric lights shine. Snow and darkness and doom can't come in here. But it was a narrow escape—from fear.

45

In the first paragraph, Pyle tells the reader that the Cumberlands are both beautiful and frightening. Mark places in the text where Pyle gives details of what contributes to the "strange fearfulness" he feels.

Authors use many techniques to create a sense of place. They may use sensory **details** and dialogue to particularize the landscape. They use comparisons and images to help you combine what you already know with the picture they are creating for you. And, they adopt a distinct **point of view** from which to describe the landscape.

Find examples of each of the techniques in "Ahead of the Night." Use the code below to mark specific passages in Ernie Pyle's newspaper column.

S = sensory details (sight, sound, smell, touch)

C = comparisons (help you visualize what might be an unfamiliar place)

P = point of view (places where Pyle explicitly reveals his point of view)

Now, draft a description of your own that will convey a sense of place. Before you write, fill in the following chart to activate your memory about the place you have selected.

Overall feeling I want to create: _____

Point of view: _____

Sight words	Sound words	Comparisons

Description of _____

Authors employ sensory and emotional details to create a sense of a place. Understanding the meaning of a text requires understanding the author's personal view of the landscape.

Two Creating a Personal View

Ernie Pyle reveals his impression of the Cumberland Mountains. At the end of the column, he says "That's what a blizzard in a Cumberland mountain valley does to a tenderfoot. The people there, I suppose, don't feel that way about it at all." His experience determined how he told the story. Experiences can also determine how we understand a story.

You have undoubtedly seen maps of the United States that emphasize different information—topography, population, state borders. Draw your own specialized map of America that emphasizes your experiences. If you have never been to certain parts of the country, you might draw clouds or just shade in that area. Think of items that represent your personal view and use them to create your map. For example, one mapmaker included a drawing of a pig for North Carolina and later explained that she had the best barbequed ribs she had ever eaten there.

Explain to a partner your personal view of the United States. Tell the stories that accompany the pictures.

Everyone has a personal view of places and events.

Three

Revealing Character

When nonfiction authors observe people, they often use the **setting** to reveal character traits or emotions. We associate certain landscapes with certain character types. Consider, for example, the stereotype of the rugged individual living on the wide open spaces of the West. By describing a person's surroundings, the writer can add to the reader's understanding of the character.

Ted Conover traveled 12,000 miles across fifteen states, living the life of a hobo and reporting his impressions. One day in California he met a woman hobo, Sheba. Jot down your initial impressions of her in the response notes.

---

from *Rolling Nowhere* by Ted Conover

←—Response notes—→

She was fifty years old and had three sons, all by different fathers ("I made some mistakes, you know"). The sons were all in their twenties; two were in the military in Texas, and she didn't know where the third was. "I always try and call 'em all at Christmas, though."

She had been dishwasher in a restaurant in Idaho, but got sick of it, and, with the boys gone, had no reason to stick around the house.

"So, I started hitchin'. Did that for a couple of years, but then I decided it was too dangerous, so I started ridin' the trains."

"The trains are safer?"

"Oh, sure, you don't get trapped in a car with some weirdo when you're ridin' freights. And I always ride alone." She had been on the road three years.

I was very surprised to learn she was fifty: she looked ten years younger, even up close, the opposite of what usually happened to the appearance of male hoboes.

"Where do you stay?" I asked. "I haven't seen you in the mission—are you up at The Pipes?" The Pipes, well known in Bakersfield tramp society, were an assortment of large water and culvert pipes strewn around an industrial lot about a half mile up the tracks; they served as an impromptu tramp motel, offering more protection from weather and intruders than did most jungle shelters.

"No, I was there for a while, but now I built me a little place. Wanta see it?"

"Sure."

We walked alongside the yards for a few minutes until Sheba stopped beside a tire-retreading plant. Tires waiting to be retreaded had spilled over the tall chain-link fence that separated it from the yards, and several hundred were piled up outside.

"Well," Sheba said, "there it is."

I strained my eyes for some kind of structure, but saw nothing. "Where?"

"Over here!" she said. She walked me toward the piles, and suddenly, amid their randomness, I saw order. Sheba had built a house, of sorts, out of automobile tires. The walls, nearly as tall as the five-foot Sheba, were composed of stacks of tires, six or seven high. Probably 150 tires had been used to construct the entire thing. The front room, which we entered through a gap in the stacks, was from *Rolling Nowhere* by Ted Conover

for cooking, sitting around the fire, and passing the time. The back room, which had a sheet metal roof, was where Sheba slept. The whole place was carpeted in cardboard. A sheet of Formica lay upon two short stacks of tires, forming the kitchen table, and was covered with food and condiments. Two buckets had been overturned for living-room chairs, with rags placed upon them for seat covers.

"Have a seat," said Sheba. "I'd offer you coffee, but I'm fresh out."

"Here, use mine," I said, astounded by this place. Sheba fanned the fire to life, made the coffee, and sat down.

"How long did this take you?" I asked.

"Oh, just a coupla hours. I made one here back a few months ago."

"How did you think of doing it?"

"Gosh, I really don't know. I think I maybe copied what my sons used to make in the back yard—you know, forts, secret hideouts."

"Nobody minds that you're here?"

"Boy, I don't think so. Who would mind? Only the tramps can see me. And not even most of them."

We finished the coffee, and Sheba announced that it was time for her nap. She had given blood the evening before, and it always tired her out. "You oughta try it, if you need the money. And why don'tcha come back by sometime?" I promised I would.

Explore the ways Sheba's character is revealed by using an inference chart. In the left column, write details of her surroundings. In the right column, write what you can infer about her.

Surroundings	Character
next to a tire-retreading plant	uses what is available; is she also "retreading" her life?
sheet of Formica	

●◆Imagine that one of Sheba's sons wants to find her. Write a description that he might give to a private detective that he has hired.

Active readers notice the details of the setting, which authors use to enrich their description of a person's character.

Four
Landscape and Identity

In a reflective essay, the writer focuses on an important aspect of experience. He or she carefully examines the experience to understand its significance better. Annie Dillard is an author who often makes connections between the place she is in and what she learns about herself and her values.

from *Pilgrim at Tinker Creek* by Annie Dillard

←—Response notes—→

Seeing is of course very much a matter of verbalization. Unless I call my attention to what passes before my eyes, I simply won't see it. If Tinker Mountain erupted, I'd be likely to notice. But if I want to notice the lesser cataclysms of valley life, I have to maintain in my head a running description of the present. It's not that I'm observant; it's just that I talk too much. Otherwise, especially in a strange place, I'll never know what's happening. Like a blind man at the ball game, I need a radio.

When I see this way I analyze and pry. I hurl over logs and roll away stones; I study the bank a square foot at a time, probing and tilting my head. Some days when a mist covers the mountains, when the muskrats won't show and the microscope's mirror shatters, I want to climb up the blank blue dome as a man would storm the inside of a circus tent, wildly, dangling, and with a steel knife claw a rent in the top, peep, and, if I must, fall.

But there is another kind of seeing that involves a letting go. When I see this way I sway transfixed and emptied. The difference between the two ways of seeing is the difference between walking with and without a camera. When I walk with a camera I walk from shot to shot, reading the light on a calibrated meter. When I walk without a camera, my own shutter opens, and the moment's light prints on my own silver gut. When I see this second way I am above all an unscrupulous observer.

It was sunny one evening last summer at Tinker Creek; the sun was low in the sky, upstream. I was sitting on the sycamore log bridge with the sunset at my back, watching the shiners the size of minnows who were feeding over the muddy sand in skittery schools. Again and again, one fish, then another, turned for a split second across the current and flash! the sun shot out from its silver side. I couldn't watch for it. It was always just happening somewhere else, and it drew my vision just as it disappeared: flash! like a sudden dazzle of the thinnest blade, a sparking over a dun and olive ground at chance intervals from every direction. Then I noticed white specks, some sort of pale petals, small, floating from under my feet on the creek's surface, very slow and steady. So I blurred my eyes and gazed toward the brim of my hat and saw a new world. I saw the pale white circles roll up, roll up, like the world's turning, mute and perfect, and I saw the linear flashes, gleaming silver, like stars being born at random down a rolling scroll of time. Something broke and something opened. I filled up like a new wineskin. I breathed an air like light; I saw a light like water. I was the lip of a fountain the creek filled

51

←—Response notes—→ forever; I was ether, the leaf in the zephyr; I was flesh-flake, feather, bone.

When I see this way I see truly. As Thoreau says, I return to my senses. I am the man who watches the baseball game in silence in an empty stadium. I see the game purely; I'm abstracted and dazed. When it's all over and the white-suited players lope off the green field to their shadowed dugouts, I leap to my feet, I cheer and cheer.

●◆ Explain how sight can lead to insight. Reread Dillard's essay and the article by Pyle in Lesson One. Consider your experiences, too, possibly referring to the personalized map you drew. Use information from your experiences and your reading to support your ideas.

52

**Understanding
how we observe our surroundings can
reveal insights into who we are.**

Five

Landscape and Values

The way that a writer describes a place is colored by personal values. The writer may speak of the "wide, open spaces" as free places where people can be themselves. Or he or she may argue that people are too concerned about being part of the "rat race" when describing a traffic jam. Critical readers must sort out the writer's values to understand the point the writer is making.

"Square Space" by Jon Roush

← Response notes →

One day a couple of years ago in Montana's Bitterroot Valley, a "domestic" bison decided it was time to head south. News reports tracked his progress. Yesterday he was seen in an irrigation ditch, today he was in someone's vegetable garden, and so on. Fences were a minor annoyance. When he did not find holes, he made them. Part Houdini, part linebacker, he let us pretend for a few days that our spaces were still wide open. If one bison could do it, why not a million? Why not one of those legendary herds that took days to pass a given point—grazing, wallowing, breeding their way across a boundless grassland? Someone finally caught the Bitterroot Bison before he reached the Divide, but it was fun while it lasted.

This winter, the state of Montana issued permits to hunt bison that strayed into Montana from Yellowstone National Park. State officials feared that the bison might carry bovine brucellosis, a virulent disease that causes cattle to abort. That Montana has been officially free from brucellosis for years is an important economic fact for cattlemen. Something had to be done. Not incidentally, the decision was applauded by hunters. The hunt was controversial with wildlife management, but surefire box office. One December evening our television sets showed us a single bison entering stage right, pausing, staggering, falling dead. He had been picked off at thirty yards by a scope-sighted hunter. Wearing camouflage fatigues in the midst of reporters, officials, and protesters, this prime-time stalker seemed overdressed. He might have sensed some absurdity himself. He told the cameras that since the hunt was legal, it must be sport.

But for deep absurdity, consider the bison's point of view. He didn't even know he had crossed a boundary. Bison, like children and other natural creatures do not bother with straight lines. They follow their interests along stream banks, around hills, from water to food to shade. That was how this Yellowstone bison was fooled. He did not have to swim any river or cross any ridge. He simply moseyed throughout the trees and across an open meadow. One minute he was in wilderness, the next—bam!—civilization. The absurdity that the bison did not understand, the absurdity that required his death, is the absurdity of laying straight lines on nature.

Yellowstone Park is square. It is square for the same reason that everything else surveyed in the Rockies is square. Our towns are laid out in square blocks, with a grid pattern of streets. Our six sections are squares, one mile on a side. Our townships are squares, six sections on a side. Our states are rectangular, except for the squiggle

53

←— Response notes —→

that follows the Continental Divide to separate Idaho and Montana. Even the northern border of the United States, after looping lyrically along eastern rivers and lakes, leaves Lake of the Woods, Minnesota, to race straight as a falling rock across swamps, plains, and mountains to the Pacific.

On a map, straight lines look logical. They imply rationality and human control. The more wild the reality, the more important the reassurance of straight lines. It's easy to understand why nineteenth-century bureaucrats and politicians, more than a thousand miles from the scene, favored them.

Back East, surveyors had used a system of land description based on meters and bounds, in which boundaries are often described in reference to actual landmarks. The western surveyor's job was to take lines already drawn on the map and lay them on the land.

This abstract, cookie-cutter space conformed to the mind of nineteenth-century America. Once it had been ruled into interchangeable squares, the vast western space could be controlled from Washington and New York. It could be, and often was, bought and sold before the actual boundaries were even laid out. It was ready for the homestead acts. It was ready to expand, township by identical township, into an empire.

Besides the abstractions of space, the other step necessary for conquering the West was the abstraction of time. Instead of measuring time by the position of the sun, phase of the moon, or season, the settlers used clocks and calendars. Precise, uniform measures of time and space allowed the coordination of complex activities separated by great distances. Above all, they allowed the development of the railroads.

And strung across the lines were the railroad towns. They were mass-produced to house the hardworking souls who bought railroad land to live on while they built the town in which they remained to create railroad markets. In Montana, Wyoming, and Idaho, some railroad towns were virtual replicas of midwestern towns already built on the same line. For them, the grid pattern was efficient as the corporate blueprints are to McDonald's.

Western towns were laid out for pure future, no past. To build a new community in the wilderness was an act of will among strangers. It was an act of will that could not afford to wait for organic growth. Boston had grown from within. Its meandering maze of streets follow the ungeometric logic of real human community. But in the western towns that were to be the settlers' new homes, history began at zero.

When you look at those old posters depicting the street plans of western towns, you can almost believe that you are looking at an established community. The town may be young, but it already has achieved its most important historical mission, imposing manmade order on the wilderness. With so much accomplished already, this is a town with a future. A good place to bring up kids.

Usually those towns arrayed themselves along a straight and endless main street. It led from the prairie, through town, and back into the prairie. In town, it was the corridor of power, and when your

54

"Square Space" by Jon Roush

← Response notes →

eyes followed it out of town, you could see the horizon. You saw the town's future prospects were infinite. A good town is still sprawling outward.

Such towns were built on the graves of bison herds and the Indians who relied on the bison for food, shelter, and clothing. In 1840, a few palisaded forts dotted an immense wilderness. Their anxious inhabitants walled out the wild. But by 1890, the towns declared victory. Without boundaries, they faded complacently into the surrounding landscape. And by the turn of the century, farms and ranchers were subduing that landscape too, with straight fence lines and the patterned order of cultivated fields.

That was why people started talking about national parks. It was time, some said, to wall the wild in, to protect it from the incursions of civilization. That way, the busy townspeople could be aware of wilderness, visit it, even revere it, without letting it interfere with business. So they put the bison in square parks and the Indians on square reservations.

But it did not end there. Bison carry brucellosis out of one park. Grizzlies lumber out of another and eat calves. Indian tribes claim water rights. At the same time, pollsters consistently find that our townspeople want more parks, more pristine water and air, more wilderness. The borders do not hold.

A hundred years ago, we would have known what to do about those stray bison. We would have rubbed out the whole herd in a weekend. Now we hesitate, uncertain. Blame nostalgia for some of the hesitation, wisdom for the rest. We have learned some humility. And we feel something missing from the compartmentalized spaces in which we have caged ourselves.

A fully civilized life includes more than law and order. It includes mystery, diversity, surprise, and beauty—the qualities that make natural space nourishing and occasionally dangerous. The rigid fragmentation of western space has walled us away from essential parts of our own being.

What do you think is the author's point in this essay?

●◆ Write a letter to Jon Roush telling him why you agree or disagree with his point. Be sure to state your view directly and use examples that make your values clear.

Sorting out the author's values is essential for understanding an argument.

Perspectives on a Subject: The American Dream

How do you make a decision when you are making a major purchase? You probably get advice from several sources—reviews from magazines, information from sales people, and recommendations from friends. You consider many different kinds of information and weigh the positive and negative features before you come to a final decision.

To understand a topic, you must also consider several perspectives. Relying on only one view can result in bias or stereotyping.

You can learn about how writers develop subjects by examining the American Dream. This idea—the dream of a better life in a new world—symbolizes both hope and despair. The early explorers of North America sought wealth. Puritans came to America for religious freedom. Settlers moved west for land. Many people paid a steep price for the financial success found in America. Mine owners became wealthy at the expense of the underpaid miners. Settlers acquired land by taking it from Native Americans. These are just a few perspectives on the idea of America.

One

Defining the Dream

Exploration of a subject often begins with a definition. Writers need to let readers know what they are discussing, especially when the subject is unfamiliar or open to several interpretations. The way an author defines the subject shapes the writing. For example, if the American Dream is seen as a dream of conquest, the author will present different situations and details than if it is viewed as a dream of freedom. Consider one writer's version of the dream.

from **"America and I"** by Anzia Yezierska

← *Response notes* →

As one of the dumb, voiceless ones I speak. One of the millions of immigrants beating, beating out their hearts at your gates for a breath of understanding.

Ach! America! From the other end of the earth where I came, America was a land of living hope, woven of dreams, aflame with longing and desire.

Choked for ages in the airless oppression of Russia, the Promised Land rose up—wings for my stifled spirit—sunlight burning through my darkness—freedom singing to me in my prison—deathless songs turning prison-bars into strings of a beautiful violin.

I arrived in America. My young, strong body, my heart and soul pregnant with the unlived lives of generations clamoring for expression.

What my mother and father and their mother and father never had a chance to give out in Russia, I would give out in America. The hidden sap of centuries would find release; colors that never saw light—songs that died unvoiced—romance that never had a chance to blossom in the black life of the Old World.

In the golden land of flowing opportunity I was to find my work that was denied me in the sterile village of my forefathers. Here I was to be free from the dead drudgery for bread that held me down in Russia. For the first time in America, I'd cease to be a slave of the belly. I'd be a creator, a giver, a human being! My work would be the living joy of fullest self-expression.

Anzia Yezierska arrived in America in 1890 with a strong desire to make a contribution in her new home. Note how she intensifies the description of her hopes by contrasting her new life with the old. Reread the selection and mark in the response notes the hopes that she had.

In the circles on the next page, write the words that she selected to describe life in the Old World and in America.

58

New World

Old World

Dreams often have a dark side, and the American Dream is no exception. Yezierska discovered that few jobs were open to her and ended up working in a sweatshop making shirtwaists. Going to college at night helped her break away, and she went on to write novels and an autobiography. Another writer, Joseph Bruchac, shows both the light and dark sides of the dream by looking at his ancestors.

59

Ellis Island
Joseph Bruchac

Beyond the red brick of Ellis Island
where the two Slovak children
who became my grandparents
waited the long days of quarantine,
after leaving the sickness,
the old Empires of Europe,
a Circle Line ship slips easily
on its way to the island
of the tall woman, green
as dreams of forests and meadows
waiting for those who'd worked
a thousand years
yet never owned their own.

Like millions of others,
I too come to this island,
nine decades the answerer
of dreams.

Response notes

Response notes

Ellis Island (continued)

Yet only one part of my blood loves that memory.
Another voice speaks
of native lands within this nation.
Lands invaded
when the earth became owned.
Lands of those who followed the changing Moon,
knowledge of the seasons
in their veins.

●◆Bruchac is descended from both immigrant and Native American families. How does he show contrasting perspectives on the American Dream? Describe each group's idea of ownership. Then, briefly explain how Bruchac uses that idea to show two sides of the American Dream.

An author's definition of a subject shapes the way he or she writes about it.

Two

Defining a Subject Through Symbols

Writers often use **symbols** to enrich their writing. They expect that readers will recognize the object they have chosen and associate meanings with it. For example, when we see an American flag, we may think of freedom. Or, we may remember people who have fought and died in wars to protect America. To millions of immigrants from Eastern Europe in the early part of the twentieth century, the Statue of Liberty near Ellis Island was the symbol of America. Reread "Ellis Island" and mark the symbols Bruchac has included.

Now, create your own symbol to define the American Dream. In the margins around the box, write words that describe your view of the American Dream. Then, draw a symbol of America in the box.

61

Discuss with a partner how your symbol represents a version of the American Dream.

When writers use symbols to develop a subject, they call upon the reader to supply additional meanings.

We all have assumptions about what we read. If we are not aware of our assumptions, we cannot read critically. We might assume that the author is telling us one thing, when he or she is really telling us something else. Poet Sherman Alexie forces us to examine our assumptions and read between the lines in the poem below. He uses **irony** to show the discrepancy between the images that many people have about Native Americans from watching old movies and the reality of Native American life today.

Response notes

Translated from the American
Sherman Alexie

after all the drive-in theaters have closed
for winter   I'll make camp alone
at THE NORTH CEDAR   replay westerns

The Seventh Cavalry riding double formation
endlessly   Main Avenue stretches
past The Union Gospel Mission   where I keep
a post office box   miles away

at my permanent address   I'll wrap myself
in old blankets   wait   for white boys
climbing fences   to watch this Indian speak

in subtitles   they'll surround me
and when they ask   "how"
I'll give them exact directions

62

To sort out the discrepancies between assumptions and reality, list three details from the poem in each category below.

Assumptions of the "white boys"	Details of the speaker's daily life
Indians "camp out"	has a permanent address

The title and last line support Alexie's ironic vision. With a partner, speculate about the possible meanings of "Translated from the American" and the double meaning of "I'll give them exact directions." Consider the ways that this poem relates to the American Dream of owning a house, having a job, and being free.

Write an explanation of how Alexie uses irony to force the reader to examine assumptions about Native Americans and the American Dream.

63

Authors challenge our assumptions about a subject in order to enlarge our understanding of it.

Satirizing the Subject

Satire is a powerful means of making readers re-examine a subject. The satirist aims to challenge some aspect of people or society through wit and humor. The satire may be gentle or biting; the target may be major or minor. Active readers need to identify the target of the satire and the aspect being satirized.

The poet E. E. Cummings is well-known for his experiments with word order, sentence structure, and punctuation. In the sonnet "next to of course god america i," Cummings satirizes certain aspects of American culture.

Response notes

next to of course god america i
E. E. Cummings

"next to of course god america i
love you land of the pilgrims' and so forth oh
say can you see by the dawn's early my
country 'tis of centuries come and go
and are no more what of it we should worry
in every language even deafanddumb
thy sons acclaim your glorious name by gorry
by jingo by gee by gosh by gum
why talk of beauty what could be more beautiful than these heroic happy dead
who rushed like lions to the roaring slaughter
they did not stop to think they died instead
then shall the voice of liberty be mute?"

He spoke. And drank rapidly a glass of water

64

Reread the poem. Underline all of the excerpts from patriotic songs or speeches you recognize. For example, "land of the pilgrims'" is from the song "America."

Cummings selected the **sonnet** form to enhance his satire. He adapted the standard **rhyme** scheme for the sonnet. If you mark the rhyming words at the end of the lines, you will notice the pattern: *ababcdcdefgfeg*.

●◆Imitate Cummings's style as you draft your own satiric sonnet. Select a topic that you feel strongly about. Have the target clearly in mind and identify one or more weaknesses that should be changed. Consider the standard phrases associated with your topic. The wording and rhyme scheme will probably be rough in this first draft but start developing your topic and your satiric perspective on it.

....	*a*
....	*b*
....	*a*
....	*b*
....	*c*
....	*d*
....	*c*
....	*d*
....	*e*
....	*f*
....	*g*
....	*f*
....	*e*
....	*g*

65

A satirical perspective on a subject reveals facets that, according to the author, should be changed.

One subtle way to develop a subject is to report on a real-life incident that exemplifies certain aspects. In a magazine article, the writer can arrange the events, dialogue, and details to create an impression. Although the story must be faithful to what really happened, the author does more than merely observe and record "the facts."

Joan Didion reveals the values inherent in the American Dream in her story about a conflict in Monterey County, California. The conflict she describes here is over how Joan Baez—singer, songwriter and anti-war protester during the 1960s and 1970s—may use land that she purchased.

from **"Where the Kissing Never Stops"** by Joan Didion

← *Response notes* →

Outside the Monterey County Courthouse in Salinas, California, the Downtown Merchants' Christmas decorations glittered in the thin sunlight that makes the winter lettuce grow. Inside, the crowd blinked uneasily in the blinding television lights. The occasion was a meeting of the Monterey County Board of Supervisors, and the issue, on this warm afternoon before Christmas 1965, was whether or not a small school in the Carmel Valley, the Institute for the Study of Nonviolence, owned by Miss Joan Baez, was in violation of Section 32-C of the Monterey County Zoning Code, which prohibits land use "detrimental to the peace, morals, or general welfare of Monterey County." Mrs. Gerald Petkuss, who lived across the road from the school, had put the problem another way. "We wonder what kind of people would go to a school like this," she asked quite early in the controversy. "Why they aren't out working and making money."

Mrs. Petkuss was a plump young matron with an air of bewildered determination, and she came to the rostrum in a strawberry-pink knit dress to say that she had been plagued "by people associated with Miss Baez's school coming up to ask where it was although they knew perfectly *well* where it was—one gentleman I remember had a beard."

"Well I don't *care*," Mrs. Petkuss cried when someone in the front row giggled. "I have three small children, that's a big responsibility, and I don't like to have to worry about . . ." Mrs. Petkuss paused delicately. "About who's around."

The hearing lasted from two until 7:15 p.m., five hours and fifteen minutes of participatory democracy during which it was suggested, on the one hand, that the Monterey County Board of Supervisors was turning our country into Nazi Germany, and, on the other, that the presence of Miss Baez and her fifteen students in the Carmel Valley would lead to "Berkeley-type" demonstrations, demoralize trainees at Fort Ord, paralyze Army convoys using the Carmel Valley road, and

from **"Where the Kissing Never Stops"** by Joan Didion

←—Response notes—→

send property values plummeting throughout the county. "Frankly, I can't conceive of anyone buying property near such an operation," declared Mrs. Petkuss's husband, who is a veterinarian. Both Dr. and Mrs. Petkuss, the latter near tears, said that they were particularly offended by Miss Baez's presence on her property during weekends. It seemed that she did not always stay inside. She sat out under trees, and walked around the property.

"We don't start until one," someone from the school objected. "Even if we did make noise, which we don't, the Petkusses could sleep until one, I don't see what the problem is."

The Petkusses' lawyer jumped up. "The *problem* is that the Petkusses happen to have a very beautiful swimming pool, they'd like to have guests out on weekends, like to use the pool."

"They'd have to stand up on a table to see the school."

"They will, too," shouted a young woman who had already indicated her approval of Miss Baez by reading aloud to the supervisors a passage from John Stuart Mill's *On Liberty*. "They'll be out with spyglasses."

"That is *not* true," Mrs. Petkuss keened. "We see the school out of three bedroom windows, out of one livingroom window, it's the only direction we can *look*."

Miss Baez sat very still in the front row. She was wearing a long-sleeved navy-blue dress with an Irish lace collar and cuffs, and she kept her hands folded in her lap. She is extraordinary looking, far more so than her photographs suggest, since the camera seems to emphasize an Indian cast to her features and fails to record either the startling fineness and clarity of her bones and eyes or, her most striking characteristic, her absolute directness, her absence of guile. She has a great natural style, and she is what used to be called a lady. "Scum," hissed an old man with a snap-on bow tie who had identified himself as "a veteran of two wars" and who is a regular at such meetings. *"Spaniel."* He seemed to be referring to the length of Miss Baez's hair, and was trying to get her attention by tapping with his walking stick, but her eyes did not flicker from the rostrum. After a while she got up, and stood until the room was completely quiet. Her opponents sat tensed, ready to spring up and counter whatever defense she was planning to make of her politics, of her school, of beards, of "Berkeley-type" demonstrations and disorder in general.

"Everybody's talking about their forty- and fifty-thousand-dollar houses and their property values going down," she drawled finally, keeping her clear voice low and gazing levelly at the supervisors. "I'd just like to say one thing. I have more than one *hundred* thousand dollars invested in the Carmel Valley, and I'm interested in protecting my property too." The property owner smiled disingenuously at Dr. and Mrs. Petkuss then, and took her seat amid complete silence.

67

Several values are evident in this selection. Complete the chart to reveal them.

Values associated with Mrs. Petkuss	Phrase or sentence that reveals the value
privacy	"We see the school out of three bedroom windows . . ."

Values associated with Ms. Baez	Phrase or sentence that reveals the value
right to own land	". . . I'm interested in protecting my property too."

➥ Whose side do you think Joan Didion is taking in this article? Explain how you determined what her views are.

Some subjects are developed through the way that an incident is presented. The writer reveals his or her views through choices about how an incident is told.

Observing and Reflecting

Writers are keen observers of their surroundings. They are always on the lookout for things that connect with an idea. By carefully describing what they have seen, they can make their ideas concrete and real. Readers, too, need to be observers. If the writing is good and the reader is observant, the reader sees what the writer has seen.

Writers sometimes act almost as if they were painters. They use what they see as the basis for writing a close study of the picture in front of them. They may even set it up, as painters set up a still life—an arrangement of things, usually fruit or flowers, perhaps a stone, a dish, or other object. When artists set up a still life, they pay attention to the background, maybe using a window for the light, or hanging a draped cloth behind the display.

Writers do the same thing. They reflect on the meaning of what they have described, expressing some idea that the image makes them think of. Artists, writers, readers—they have a lot in common, and that commonality has to do with observing and reflecting.

One — Reflecting on a Small Event

Read Robert Frost's poem "Dust of Snow," taking note of what actually happens and how this small event affects him.

Response notes

Dust of Snow
Robert Frost

The way a crow
Shook down on me
The dust of snow
From a hemlock tree

Has given my heart
A change of mood
And saved some part
Of a day I had rued.

Think of three or four small things that happened to you recently. List them in the chart below. Beside each event, note some surrounding details. Try to recall what this event made you think about or how it made you feel.

Event	Surrounding details	Thoughts or feelings

Choose one of these events and write a short poem, modeled loosely on "Dust of Snow." Describe the event in the first part of your poem. Then, in the second part, tell how the event affected you. Keep the lines short. If you want to, you can follow Frost's example of alternate rhymes.

Poets' observations of simple, everyday events often provide subjects for their poems.

Read Sylvia Plath's poem "Black Rook in Rainy Weather," making note of your responses. A rook is a bird in the crow or raven family.

Response notes

Black Rook in Rainy Weather
Sylvia Plath

On the stiff twig up there
Hunches a wet black rook
Arranging and rearranging its feathers in the rain.
I do not expect miracle
Or an accident

To set the sight on fire
In my eye, nor seek
Any more in the desultory weather some design,
But let spotted leaves fall as they fall,
Without ceremony, or portent.

Although, I admit, I desire,
Occasionally, some backtalk
From the mute sky, I can't honestly complain:
A certain minor light may still
Leap incandescent

Out of kitchen table or chair
As if a celestial burning took
Possession of the most obtuse objects now and then—
Thus hallowing an interval
Otherwise inconsequent

By bestowing largesse, honour,
One might say love. At any rate, I now walk
Wary (for it could happen
Even in this dull, ruinous landscape); skeptical,
Yet politic; ignorant

Of whatever angel may choose to flare
Suddenly at my elbow. I only know that a rook
Ordering its black feathers can so shine
As to seize my senses, haul
My eyelids up, and grant

A brief respite from fear
Of total neutrality. With luck,
Trekking stubborn through this season
Of fatigue, I shall
Patch together a content

Of sorts. Miracles occur,
If you care to call those spasmodic
Tricks of radiance miracles. The wait's begun again,
The long wait for the angel,
For that rare, random descent.

Frost's response to his experience with a crow resulted in a straightforward, simple poem. Plath, on the other hand, observes a simple event—a rook "ordering its black feathers"—and engages in a lengthy, philosophical reflection.

●◆ Look for the sections of Plath's poem that deal specifically with the event that stimulates the poem. Write these passages below. Then paraphrase her reflections.

Passages dealing with Plath's observations	Paraphrase of her reflections about these observations

73

●⌐ Look back at the poem you drafted in the previous lesson. Write a new version of the poem—it should be a longer, more extended reflection about the same event. Let your imagination go. Take the meaning of this event as far as you can stretch it. Model your new poem after Plath's.

In reading a philosophical poem, it is helpful to keep in mind the initial observation that inspired the poem.

Three
Deceptively Simple

Jane Kenyon lived in New Hampshire with her husband Donald Hall, also a poet.

Otherwise
Jane Kenyon

I got out of bed
on two strong legs.
It might have been
otherwise. I ate
cereal, sweet
milk, ripe, flawless
peach. It might
have been otherwise.
I took the dog uphill
to the birch wood.
All morning I did
the work I love.

At noon I lay down
with my mate. It might
have been otherwise.
We ate dinner together
at a table with silver
candlesticks. It might
have been otherwise.
I slept in a bed
in a room with paintings
on the walls, and
planned another day
just like this day.
But one day, I know,
it will be otherwise.

Response notes

75

➦ At first glance, this poem seems to be a simple list of daily events in the writer's life. There is nothing unusual, nothing unexpected in the sequence from morning to night. Explain how the repeated line "It might have been otherwise" transforms this poem into a reflection on the importance of the small, everyday events that order her life. Pay special attention to the last two lines.

●◆ List five or six things that you do each day, almost without thinking about them.

●◆ Now strip these events down to bare statements. After each one, insert Kenyon's line "It might have been otherwise." Write out your lines with the refrain so that it takes the same form as Kenyon's poem.

Some poems seem simple on the surface, but have deeper meanings. Poets may signal these meanings by using a refrain that takes on new meaning by the end of the poem.

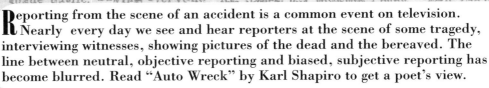

Four
The Poet as Reporter

Reporting from the scene of an accident is a common event on television. Nearly every day we see and hear reporters at the scene of some tragedy, interviewing witnesses, showing pictures of the dead and the bereaved. The line between neutral, objective reporting and biased, subjective reporting has become blurred. Read "Auto Wreck" by Karl Shapiro to get a poet's view.

Auto Wreck
Karl Shapiro

Response notes

Its quick soft silver bell beating, beating,
And down the dark one ruby flare
Pulsing out red light like an artery,
The ambulance at top speed floating down
Past beacons and illuminated clocks
Wings in a heavy curve, dips down,
And brakes speed, entering the crowd.
The doors leap open, emptying light;
Stretchers are laid out, the mangled lifted
And stowed into the little hospital.
Then the bell, breaking the hush, tolls once,
And the ambulance with its terrible cargo
Rocking, slightly rocking, moves away,
As the doors, an afterthought, are closed.

We are deranged, walking among the cops
Who sweep glass and are large and composed.
One is still making notes under the light.
One with a bucket douches ponds of blood
Into the street and gutter.
One hangs lanterns on the wrecks that cling,
Empty husks of locusts, to iron poles.

Our throats were tight as tourniquets,
Our feet were bound with splints, but now,
Like convalescents intimate and gauche,
We speak through sickly smiles and warn
With the stubborn saw of common sense,
The grim joke and the banal resolution.
The traffic moves around with care,
But we remain, touching a wound
That opens to our richest horror.

Already old, the question Who shall die?
Becomes unspoken Who is innocent?
For death in war is done by hands;
Suicide has cause and stillbirth, logic;
And cancer, simple as a flower, blooms.

But this invites the occult mind,
Cancels our physics with a sneer,
And spatters all we knew of denouement
Across the expedient and wicked stones.

77

Reread the poem and focus on three elements: the narrator's actual observations, the narrator's reactions to the scene, and the narrator's reflections on what he has witnessed.

●◆ Write key words and phrases for each of the elements in the chart below.

Narrator's observations	Narrator's reactions	Narrator's reflections

●◆ How would a television reporter present this scene? What would be omitted? added? Write a short description of this accident as a reporter might report it.

Like journalists, poets must observe, select, and present. At the end of the "broadcast," they, too, very often include a reflective comment.

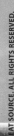

The poet Wallace Stevens presents in some of his poems what artists call a still life, an arrangement of objects on a specific background. As you read this poem, picture a painting of the pears in your mind: the green cloth providing the surface, the pears arranged so that there is shadow. Do not be put off by the first line; it is just the scientific name for pears.

Study of Two Pears
Wallace Stevens

I

Opusculum paedagogum.
The pears are not viols,
Nudes or bottles.
They resemble nothing else.

II

They are yellow forms
Composed of curves
Bulging toward the base.
They are touched red.

III

They are not flat surfaces
Having curved outlines.
They are round
Tapering toward the top.

IV

In the way they are modelled
There are bits of blue.
A hard dry leaf hangs
From the stem.

V

The yellow glistens.
It glistens with various yellows,
Citrons, oranges and greens
Flowering over the skin.

VI

The shadows of the pears
Are blobs on the green cloth.
The pears are not seen
As the observer wills.

Response notes

Poets observe objects by noting what is not there as well as what is. Distinguish the two methods of description below.

Descriptions of what the pears actually look like	Statements about what the pears are not

●◆ Write your thoughts about what you think Stevens means by the last two lines. In your response, consider the poet as a careful observer and as a reflective thinker. If you wish, illustrate your response by sketching the still life as Stevens has represented it.

Poets must observe the objects of their study as closely as scientists do. Close study enhances the believability of conclusions and reflections.

Evaluating Poems

We have all heard people say, "It's just like comparing apples and oranges." The implication is that you cannot compare the two because they are different items. The truth is, of course, that you can compare, perhaps comparing the amounts of Vitamin C each possesses or the amount of fiber or some other nutritional benefit. But you cannot criticize an orange for not being an apple. To judge the quality of one orange, you have to set up criteria that apply only to oranges. Then you can say, with confidence, that this orange is a better orange for juice, while that one is better for making marmalade.

The same thinking holds true for all evaluations. Making judgments is central to our thinking. We are always judging: people, movies, schools, clothes, teachers. What we often forget is that we can only judge a thing with validity if we have set up criteria. And, once we have made a judgment, we need to support it with evidence that is accu-rate, sensible, and valid. Only then can we hope to persuade others to our point of view.

The poem "Sisyphus" by Josephine Miles is based on an ancient Greek **myth**. Sisyphus is in Hades, condemned eternally to roll a great boulder up a mountain, only to have it roll back down again. The true punishment is that Sisyphus is aware, as he is rolling it up, that it will roll back down. Read Miles's poem to see how she uses the myth for her own purposes.

Response notes

Sisyphus
Josephine Miles

When Sisyphus was pushing the stone up the
   mountain,
Always near the top
As you remember, at the very tip of the height,
It lapsed and fell back upon him,
And he rolled to the bottom of the incline,
   exhausted.

Then he got up and pushed up the stone again,
First over the grassy rise, then the declivity of
   dead man's gulch,
Then the outcroppings halfway, at which he
   took breath,
Looking out over the rosy panorama of Helicon;
Then finally the top

Where the stone wobbled, trembled, and lapsed
   back upon him,
And he rolled again down the whole incline.
Why?
He said a man's reach must exceed his grasp,
Or what is Hades for?

He said it's not the goal that matters, but the
   process
Of reaching it, the breathing joy
Of endeavor, and the labor along the way.
This belief damned him, and damned, what's
   harder,
The heavy stone.

82

To evaluate a poem, you need to establish criteria. Begin your evaluation with the question of Miles's use of myth. First, ask a question about the myth. Example: "How effective is Miles's use of the story of Sisyphus in conveying the real point of her poem?" To answer this question, clarify what you see as the point of the poem; then support your judgment with quotations from the poem. This exercise might be termed "Notes for an Evaluation Essay."

●◆ Write notes for this assignment here:

1. What do you see to be the point of the poem?

2. How effective is the poem?

83

3. Support your judgment about the effectiveness of Miles's use of the myth of Sisyphus with quotations from the poem.

Evaluating the effectiveness of a poem in terms of one criterion provides a start toward building an interpretation.

R ead "The Mountain" by Louise Glück, which is also based on the myth of Sisyphus. Again, read it the first time for meaning.

Response notes

The Mountain
Louise Glück

My students look at me expectantly.
I explain to them that the life of art is a life
of endless labor. Their expressions
hardly change; they need to know
a little more about endless labor.
So I tell them the story of Sisyphus,
how he was doomed to push
a rock up a mountain, knowing nothing
would come of this effort
but that he would repeat it
indefinitely. I tell them
there is joy in this, in the artist's life,
that one eludes
judgment, and as I speak
I am secretly pushing a rock myself,
slyly pushing it up the steep
face of a mountain. Why do I lie
to these children? They aren't listening,
they aren't deceived, their fingers
tapping at the wooden desks—
So I retract
the myth; I tell them it occurs
in hell, and that the artist lies
because he is obsessed with attainment,
that he perceives the summit
as that place where he will live forever,
a place about to be
transformed by his burden: with every breath,
I am standing at the top of the mountain.
Both my hands are free. And the rock has added
height to the mountain.

●◆ What do you think this poem is about?

....

....

....

●◆ Since the Glück poem is based on the same myth as the one Josephine Miles wrote, use the same question to set up your judgment about it: "How effective is Glück's use of the story of Sisyphus in conveying the real point of her poem?" Again, clarify what you see to be the point of the poem, then support your judgment with quotations from the poem.

1. What do you see to be the point of the poem?

2. How effective is the poem?

85

3. Support your judgment about the effectiveness of Glück's use of the Sisyphus myth with quotations from the poem.

Applying the same criterion to two poems is the basis for a comparison of the two poems.

Three

Comparing Two Poems

Comparing two poems makes your judgment of both more effective. Fill out the chart below to gather information for evaluating the two poems about Sisyphus.

Things to compare	"Sisyphus" by Josephine Miles	"The Mountain" by Louise Glück
How does the poem make me feel?		
What can I say about the language of the poem?		
How easy or hard is it to understand?		
What lines really stand out in the poem?		

The question now is "Which poem is more effective in its use of the Sisyphus myth in conveying the real point of the poem?" Make a judgment. Then, use material from the chart to support your judgment. Be sure to use quotations from both poems to support your ideas.

Which poem is more effective?

....

....

Support for your judgment:

....

....

....

....

....

....

....

....

....

....

....

....

....

....

....

....

....

....

....

....

87

Comparing two poems gives you the opportunity to make valid judgments based on selected criteria.

Read "Dog's Death" by John Updike. In the margins, note your responses to the poem.

Response notes

Dog's Death
John Updike

She must have been kicked unseen or brushed by a car.
Too young to know much, she was beginning to learn
To use the newspapers spread on the kitchen floor
And to win, wetting there, the words, "Good dog!
                                             Good dog!"

We thought her shy malaise was a shot reaction.
The autopsy disclosed a rupture in her liver.
As we teased her with play, blood was filling her skin
And her heart was learning to lie down forever.

Monday morning, as the children were noisily fed
And sent to school, she crawled beneath the youngster's bed.
We found her twisted and limp but still alive.
In the car to the vet's, on my lap, she tried

To bite my hand and died. I stroked her warm fur
And my wife called in a voice imperious with tears.
Though surrounded by love that would have upheld her,
Nevertheless she sank and, stiffening, disappeared.

Back home, we found that in the night her frame,
Drawing near to dissolution, had endured the shame
of diarrhea and had dragged across the floor
To a newspaper carelessly left there. *Good dog.*

Sentiment and sentimentality—these two words look very much alike, but their meanings differ. In poetry, we look for sentiment, an honest expression of emotion in keeping with the occasion or subject of the poem. In poems with sentiment, emotion is evoked by concrete language with specific detail. Sentimentality results from the evoking of emotion that is excessive for the occasion. In poems with sentimentality, there is often a good deal of talking about the emotion, a heavy use of clichés and of **abstract** words like *love* or *beauty*. Here are some questions that will help you look at this distinction. Discuss these with a partner and jot down your responses.

●◆ What is the dominant emotion of the poem?

88

●◆ What is the effect of using such unusual words as *malaise* (a vague feeling of illness or depression) and *dissolution* (disintegration or death)?

Now look closely at the language of the poem. In the chart below, list words that you think describe honest sentiment and those that you think are excessive. (You may not have words in both columns.) Then explain your choices.

Words that evoke sentiment	Words that lead to sentimentality	Reasons for my choices

●◆ Review your notes about Updike's poem and decide whether the poem is evoking sentiment that is justified by the occasion or whether it is sentimental. Include evidence for your decision. Remember that a powerful emotional response to a poem does not mean that the poem is sentimental.

When judging a poem's use of sentiment, as opposed to sentimentality, a good reader looks at the poet's language. Concrete language with specific detail creates stronger emotional responses than flowery, overblown abstractions.

89

Five

Precise Diction

In writing, the word **diction** simply means "choice in use of words." Precise diction means the words used are exactly appropriate to the occasion or situation. Precise diction is an important characteristic of effective poetry. It does not require the use of big words or unusual words unless such words are called for by the occasion of the poem. A poet can use **slang** or **dialect**, for example, and be extremely effective. When evaluating a poem, we, as readers, need to look carefully at the writer's diction and decide whether the words are effective.

Response notes

The Great Blue Heron
Carolyn Kizer

As I wandered on the beach
I saw the heron standing
Sunk in the tattered wings
He wore as a hunchback's coat.
Shadow without a shadow,
Hung on invisible wires
From the top of a canvas day,
What scissors cut him out?
Superimposed on a poster
Of summer by the strand
Of a long-decayed resort,
Poised in the dusty light
Some fifteen summers ago;
I wondered, an empty child,
"Heron, whose ghost are you?"

I stood on the beach alone,
In the sudden chill of the burned.
My thought raced up the path.
Pursuing it, I ran
To my mother in the house
And led her to the scene.
The spectral bird was gone.

But her quick eye saw him drifting
Over the highest pines
On vast, unmoving wings.
Could they be those ashen things,
So grounded, unwieldy, ragged,
A pair of broken arms
That were not made for flight?
In the middle of my loss
I realized she knew:
My mother knew what he was.

O great blue heron, now
That the summer house has burned
So many rockets ago,
So many smokes and fires
And beach-lights and water-glow
Reflecting pin-wheel and flare:
The old logs hauled away,
The pines and driftwood cleared
From that bare strip of shore
Where dozens of children play;
Now there is only you
Heavy upon my eye.
Why have you followed me here,
Heavy and far away?
You have stood there patiently
For fifteen summers and snows,
Denser than my repose,
Bleaker than any dream,
Waiting upon the day
When, like gray smoke, a vapor
Floating into the sky,
A handful of paper ashes,
My mother would drift away.

91

Precise diction enables poets to be economical in their language. Ideas that might take only a few lines in a poem take much longer in prose. Writing a paraphrase enables you to get a sense of the precision and economy of language. For example, lines 15–22 of "The Great Blue Heron" might be paraphrased this way:

"Heron, whose ghost are you?"

I stood on the beach alone,
In the sudden chill of the burned.
My thought raced up the path.
Pursuing it, I ran
To my mother in the house
And led her to the scene.
The spectral bird was gone.

I found myself talking to the bird that was standing on the beach. I felt as if I were seeing a ghost. I was standing there alone. Suddenly, I experienced the feeling of being both chilled and burned at the same time. My thoughts were racing. I wanted my mother to come see this bird. I ran up the path to my mother in the house and told her to come look at the bird on the beach. But when we got there, the ghost-like bird was gone.

Underline the key words in the passage below. Key words are words that are important to the meaning, either realistic or symbolic. For example, you might underline *fifteen*, which explains the distance in time from the event to the reflection. Then try your hand at paraphrasing the lines:

Paraphrase

Now there is only you

Heavy upon my eye.

Why have you followed me here,

Heavy and far away?

You have stood there patiently

For fifteen summers and snows,

Denser than my repose,

Bleaker than any dream,

Waiting upon the day

When, like gray smoke, a vapor

Floating into the sky,

A handful of paper ashes,

My mother would drift away.

●◆ Compare your paraphrase with that of a partner. Notice how they are alike or different. Where they are different, explain your thinking to your partner. Remember that we bring different knowledge to our reading, so it is natural that there will be variations in our interpretations.

How effective is the language in Kizer's "The Great Blue Heron"? Remember that in constructing an evaluation, you must:

1. establish your criteria.

2. make a judgment.

3. support it by referring to the poem.

92

Precise diction is one of the most important characteristics of a good poem

Focus on the Writer: Truman Capote

In 1984, Truman Capote ironically summed up his life and career in a conversation with his biographer, Gerald Clarke: "There's the one and only T. C. There was nobody like me before, and there ain't gonna be anybody like me after I'm gone."

This singular man was raised by elderly relatives in rural Alabama during the Depression. At age ten he moved to New York City to live with his mother and her new husband.

His first story was published when he was seventeen and he became famous at age 24 with the publication of his first novel *Other Voices, Other Rooms* in 1948. This was followed by a series of successful novels, stories, movie scripts, and magazine articles.

In 1959, Capote began researching the murders of a farmer and his family in a small Kansas farm town. His minutely-reconstructed account of the murders and their aftermath was published in 1966 as *In Cold Blood*. With it, Capote could claim to have invented a new form of literature, the nonfiction novel. Although some critics question the newness of the form, most agree that *In Cold Blood* is his greatest work. Throughout all of his writing, Capote displayed a talent for capturing the essence of people and places.

Truman Capote was a careful craftsman, always searching for just the right word to achieve the effect he wanted. Newspaper columnist Herb Caen tells about an evening with author Robert Ruark and Capote. Ruark said, "I wrote five thousand words today, Truman, and I bet you sat there at that desk with your quill pen and wrote one word." Truman said, "Yes, Robert, but it was the right word." Capote attributed his ability to talent rather than hard work. He told interviewer Lawrence Grobel, "I've known all my life I could take a bunch of words and throw them up in the air and they would come down just right. I'm a semantic Paganini."

➥ Stop and consider for a moment what these anecdotes reveal about Capote's writing. What does he imply when he compares himself to the celebrated virtuoso violinist Paganini?

....

....

....

Now read Capote's description of jazz musician Louis Armstrong. Note the specific words and phrases he uses. He characterizes not only the musician but also establishes a time and place. Mark the phrases in the text that evoke character, time, and place for you.

"Louis Armstrong" from *Observations* by Truman Capote

←—Response notes—→

Surely the Satch has forgotten, still, he was one of this writer's first friends, I met him when I was four, that would be around 1928, and he, a hard-plump and belligerently happy brown Buddha, was playing aboard a pleasure steamer that paddled between New Orleans and St. Louis. Never mind why, but I had occasion to take the trip very often, and for me the sweet anger of Armstrong's trumpet, the froggy exuberance of his come-to-me-baby mouthings, are a piece of Proust's madeleine cake: they make Mississippi moons rise again, summon the muddy lights of river towns, the sound, like an alligator's yawn, of river horns—I hear the rush of the mulatto river pushing by, hear, always, stomp! stomp! the beat of the grinning Buddha's foot as he shouts his way into "Sunny Side of the Street" and the honeymooning dancers, dazed with bootleg brew and sweating through their talcum, bunny-hug around the ship's saloony ballroom. The Satch, he was good to me, he told me I had talent, that I ought to be in vaudeville; he gave me a bamboo cane and a straw boater with a peppermint headband; and every night from the stand announced: "Ladies and gentlemen, now we're going to present you one of America's nice kids, he's going to do a little tap dance." Afterward I passed among the passengers, collecting in my hat nickels and dimes. This went on all summer, I grew rich and vain; but in October the river roughened, the moon whitened, the customers lessened, the boat rides ended, and with them my career. Six years later, while living at

"Louis Armstrong" from *Observations* by Truman Capote

a boarding school from which I wanted to run away, I wrote my
former, now famous, benefactor, and said if I came to New York,
couldn't he get me a job at the Cotton Club or somewhere? There was
no reply, maybe he never got the letter, it doesn't matter, I still loved
him, still do.

←———Response notes———→

In the broadest sense, **local color** writing employs details of the **dialect**, dress,
customs, and scenery to portray a specific region of the United States. Capote
resisted being categorized as a Southern writer. In fact, most of his stories were not
set in the South. Yet he was able to draw the reader into specific times and places
through the details he chose. Look back at the words and phrases you marked in
"Louis Armstrong." Explain what three of them suggest in the chart below.

Word or phrase	Effect
example: an alligator's yawn	something deep, primitive, even dangerous
1.	1.
2.	2.
3.	3.

95

●◆ Write a brief sketch of a person you know well. You need not know him or her
personally, but choose someone that you can characterize with specific words and
phrases. Include local color details to establish time and place.

Writers
enhance their
writing with
carefully chosen
details that place
the reader in a
specific time
and place.

Two Dualities

Truman Capote's work often emphasized the dualities in life—light and dark, good and evil, dream and nightmare. His short story "Miriam" was published in *Mademoiselle* magazine in 1945 and won the O. Henry Memorial Award in 1946. In it, you can find many of the characteristics of Capote's style. Read the first part of the story to get a sense of the contrasts he creates between characters.

"Miriam" by Truman Capote

← *Response notes* →

For several years, Mrs. H. T. Miller had lived alone in a pleasant apartment (two rooms with kitchenette) in a remodeled brownstone near the East River. She was a widow: Mr. H. T. Miller had left a reasonable amount of insurance. Her interests were narrow, she had no friends to speak of, and she rarely journeyed farther than the corner grocery. The other people in the house never seemed to notice her: her clothes were matter-of-fact, her hair iron-gray, clipped and casually waved; she did not use cosmetics, her features were plain and inconspicuous, and on her last birthday she was sixty-one. Her activities were seldom spontaneous: she kept the two rooms immaculate, smoked an occasional cigarette, prepared her own meals and tended a canary.

Then she met Miriam. It was snowing that night. Mrs. Miller had finished drying the supper dishes and was thumbing through an afternoon paper when she saw an advertisement of a picture playing at a neighborhood theater. The title sounded good, so she struggled into her beaver coat, laced her galoshes and left the apartment, leaving one light burning in the foyer: she found nothing more disturbing than a sensation of darkness.

The snow was fine, falling gently, not yet making an impression on the pavement. The wind from the river cut only at street crossings. Mrs. Miller hurried, her head bowed, oblivious as a mole burrowing a blind path. She stopped at a drugstore and bought a package of peppermints.

A long line stretched in front of the box office; she took her place at the end. There would be (a tired voice groaned) a short wait for all seats. Mrs. Miller rummaged in her leather handbag till she collected exactly the correct change for admission. The line seemed to be taking its own time and, looking around for some distraction, she suddenly became conscious of a little girl standing under the edge of the marquee.

Her hair was the longest and strangest Mrs. Miller had ever seen: absolutely silver-white, like an albino's. It flowed waist-length in smooth, loose lines. She was thin and fragilely constructed. There was a simple, special elegance in the way she stood with her thumbs in the pockets of a tailored plum-velvet coat.

Mrs. Miller felt oddly excited, and when the little girl glanced toward her, she smiled warmly. The little girl walked over and said, "Would you care to do me a favor?"

"I'd be glad to, if I can," said Mrs. Miller.

"Miriam" by Truman Capote

←—Response notes—→

"Oh, it's quite easy. I merely want you to buy a ticket for me; they won't let me in otherwise. Here, I have the money." And gracefully she handed Mrs. Miller two dimes and a nickel.

They went over to the theater together. An usherette directed them to a lounge; in twenty minutes the picture would be over.

"I feel just like a genuine criminal," said Mrs. Miller gaily, as she sat down. "I mean, that sort of thing's against the law, isn't it? I do hope I haven't done the wrong thing. Your mother knows where you are, dear? I mean she does, doesn't she?"

The little girl said nothing. She unbuttoned her coat and folded it across her lap. Her dress underneath was prim and dark blue. A gold chain dangled about her neck, and her fingers, sensitive and musical-looking, toyed with it. Examining her more attentively, Mrs. Miller decided the truly distinctive feature was not her hair, but her eyes; they were hazel, steady, lacking any childlike quality whatsoever and, because of their size, seemed to consume her small face.

Mrs. Miller offered a peppermint. "What's your name, dear?"

"Miriam," she said, as though, in some curious way, it were information already familiar.

"Why, isn't that funny—my name's Miriam, too. And it's not a terribly common name either. Now, don't tell me your last name's Miller!"

"Just Miriam."

"But isn't that funny?"

"Moderately," said Miriam, and rolled the peppermint on her tongue.

Mrs. Miller flushed and shifted uncomfortably. "You have such a large vocabulary for such a little girl."

"Do I?"

"Well, yes," said Mrs. Miller, hastily changing the topic to: "Do you like the movies?"

"I really wouldn't know," said Miriam. "I've never been before."

Women began filling the lounge; the rumble of the newsreel bombs exploded in the distance. Mrs. Miller rose, tucking her purse under her arm. "I guess I'd better be running now if I want to get a seat," she said. "It was nice to have met you."

Miriam nodded ever so slightly.

We know that Miriam and Mrs. Miller have one characteristic in common—their first name. What are their contrasting characteristics?

Miriam	Mrs. Miller
stood with a "simple, special elegance"	trip to theater is compared to a "mole burrowing a blind path"

➡◆ Select one characteristic of either Miriam or Mrs. Miller and explain what the contrast reveals. What is beneath the surface? For example, describing Mrs. Miller as a blind mole suggests that Mrs. Miller may not be aware of everything that is going on around her. Miriam, on the other hand, seems to know quite a lot for a little girl.

Contrast is one of the strongest ways to describe characters in literature.

Three
Subtle Description

Capote was well-known for his ability to create characters. He brought them to life through **dialogue**, **setting**, and action rather than description. He was a master at subtly showing their weaknesses by revealing the secrets that made them vulnerable to others. So far Miriam and Mrs. Miller seem like people we might meet anywhere. But read the next segment of the story.

"Miriam" (continued) by Truman Capote

←— Response notes —→

It snowed all week. Wheels and footsteps moved soundlessly on the street, as if the business of living continued secretly behind a pale but impenetrable curtain. In the falling quiet there was no sky or earth, only snow lifting in the wind, frosting the window glass, chilling the rooms, deadening and hushing the city. At all hours it was necessary to keep a lamp lighted, and Mrs. Miller lost track of the days: Friday was no different from Saturday and on Sunday she went to the grocery: closed, of course.

That evening she scrambled eggs and fixed a bowl of tomato soup. Then, after putting on a flannel robe and cold-creaming her face, she propped herself up in bed with a hot-water bottle under her feet. She was reading the *Times* when the doorbell rang. At first she thought it must be a mistake and whoever it was would go away. But it rang and rang and settled to a persistent buzz. She looked at the clock: a little after eleven; it did not seem possible, she was always asleep by ten.

Climbing out of bed, she trotted barefoot across the living room. "I'm coming, please be patient." The latch was caught; she turned it this way and that way and the bell never paused an instant. "Stop it," she cried. The bolt gave way and she opened the door an inch. "What in heaven's name?"

"Hello," said Miriam.

"Oh . . . why, hello," said Mrs. Miller, stepping hesitantly into the hall. "You're that little girl."

"I thought you'd never answer, but I kept my finger on the button; I knew you were home. Aren't you glad to see me?"

Mrs. Miller did not know what to say. Miriam, she saw, wore the same plum-velvet coat and now she had also a beret to match; her white hair was braided in two shining plaits and looped at the ends with enormous white ribbons.

"Since I've waited so long, you could at least let me in," she said.

"It's awfully late. . . ."

Miriam regarded her blankly. "What difference does that make? Let me in. It's cold out here and I have on a silk dress." Then, with a gentle gesture, she urged Mrs. Miller aside and passed into the apartment.

She dropped her coat and beret on a chair. She was indeed wearing a silk dress. White silk. White silk in February. The skirt was beautifully pleated and the sleeves long; it made a faint rustle as she strolled about the room. "I like your place," she said. "I like the rug, blue's my favorite color." She touched a paper rose in a vase on the

99

coffee table. "Imitation," she commented wanly. "How sad. Aren't imitations sad?" She seated herself on the sofa, daintily spreading her skirt.

"What do you want?" asked Mrs. Miller.

"Sit down," said Miriam. "It makes me nervous to see people stand."

Mrs. Miller sank to a hassock. "What do you want?" she repeated.

"You know, I don't think you're glad I came."

For a second time Mrs. Miller was without an answer; her hand motioned vaguely. Miriam giggled and pressed back on a mound of chintz pillows. Mrs. Miller observed that the girl was less pale than she remembered; her cheeks were flushed.

"How did you know where I lived?"

Miriam frowned. "That's no question at all. What's your name? What's mine?"

"But I'm not listed in the phone book."

"Oh, let's talk about something else."

Mrs. Miller said, "Your mother must be insane to let a child like you wander around at all hours of the night—and in such ridiculous clothes. She must be out of her mind."

Miriam got up and moved to a corner where a covered birdcage hung from a ceiling chain. She peeked beneath the cover. "It's a canary," she said. "Would you mind if I woke him? I'd like to hear him sing."

"Leave Tommy alone," said Mrs. Miller anxiously. "Don't you dare wake him."

"Certainly," said Miriam. "But I don't see why I can't hear him sing." And then, "Have you anything to eat? I'm starving! Even milk and a jam sandwich would be fine."

"Look," said Mrs. Miller, arising from the hassock, "look—if I make some nice sandwiches will you be a good child and run along home? It's past midnight, I'm sure."

"It's snowing," reproached Miriam. "And cold and dark."

"Well, you shouldn't have come here to begin with," said Mrs. Miller, struggling to control her voice. "I can't help the weather. If you want anything to eat, you'll have to promise to leave."

Miriam brushed a braid against her cheek. Her eyes were thoughtful, as if weighing the proposition. She turned toward the birdcage. "Very well," she said, "I promise."

How old is she? Ten? Eleven? Mrs. Miller, in the kitchen, unsealed a jar of strawberry preserves and cut four slices of bread. She poured a glass of milk and paused to light a cigarette. *And why has she come?* Her hand shook as she held the match, fascinated, till it burned her finger. The canary was singing; singing as he did in the morning and at no other time. "Miriam," she called, "Miriam, I told you not to disturb Tommy." There was no answer. She called again; all she heard was the canary. She inhaled the cigarette and discovered she had lighted the cork-tip end and—oh, really, she mustn't lose her temper.

She carried the food in on a tray and set it on the coffee table. She saw first that the birdcage still wore its night cover. And Tommy was

"Miriam" by Truman Capote

singing. It gave her a queer sensation. And no one was in the room. Mrs. Miller went through an alcove leading to her bedroom; at the door she caught her breath.

"What are you doing?" she asked.

Miriam glanced up and in her eyes there was a look that was not ordinary. She was standing by the bureau, a jewel case opened before her. For a minute she studied Mrs. Miller, forcing their eyes to meet, and she smiled. "There's nothing good here," she said. "But I like this." Her hand held a cameo brooch. "It's charming."

"Suppose—perhaps you'd better put it back," said Mrs. Miller, feeling suddenly the need of some support. She leaned against the door frame; her head was unbearably heavy; a pressure weighted the rhythm of her heartbeat. The light seemed to flutter defectively. "Please, child—a gift from my husband . . ."

"But it's beautiful and I want it," said Miriam. "*Give it to me.*"

As she stood, striving to shape a sentence which would somehow save the brooch, it came to Mrs. Miller there was no one to whom she might turn; she was alone; a fact that had not been among her thoughts for a long time. Its sheer emphasis was stunning. But here in her own room in the hushed snow-city were evidences she could not ignore or, she knew with startling clarity, resist.

Miriam ate ravenously, and when the sandwiches and milk were gone, her fingers made cobweb movements over the plate, gathering crumbs. The cameo gleamed on her blouse, the blond profile like a trick reflection of its wearer. "That was very nice," she sighed, "though now an almond cake or a cherry would be ideal. Sweets are lovely, don't you think?"

Mrs. Miller was perched precariously on the hassock, smoking a cigarette. Her hairnet had slipped lopsided and loose strands straggled down her face. Her eyes were stupidly concentrated on nothing and her cheeks were mottled in red patches, as though a fierce slap had left permanent marks.

"Is there a candy—a cake?"

Mrs. Miller tapped ash on the rug. Her head swayed slightly as she tried to focus her eyes. "You promised to leave if I made the sandwiches," she said.

"Dear me, did I?"

"It was a promise and I'm tired and I don't feel well at all."

"Mustn't fret," said Miriam. "I'm only teasing."

She picked up her coat, slung it over her arm, and arranged her beret in front of a mirror. Presently she bent close to Mrs. Miller and whispered, "Kiss me good night."

"Please—I'd rather not," said Mrs. Miller.

Miriam lifted a shoulder, arched an eyebrow. "As you like," she said, and went directly to the coffee table, seized the vase containing the paper roses, carried it to where the hard surface of the floor lay bare, and hurled it downward. Glass sprayed in all directions and she stamped her foot on the bouquet.

Then slowly she walked to the door, but before closing it, she looked back at Mrs. Miller with a slyly innocent curiosity.

●◆You can see how the relationship between Miriam and Mrs. Miller is developing. Return to the text and mark the places where Capote shows Miriam gaining power over Mrs. Miller. Then, write your ideas about this question: What character weakness allows Mrs. Miller to lose control?

Writers
can develop plots
through subtle
indications of the
strengths and
weaknesses of a
character.

Four

Gothic Style

Capote's early stories, like "Miriam," shared some characteristics of the **gothic style** of Edgar Allan Poe and Nathaniel Hawthorne. In their works, dark and gloomy settings provided the backdrop for terrifying, even supernatural events. Yet, the terror in a Capote story generally arises from the weaknesses of a character rather than a supernatural force. With a mixture of dream, fantasy, and reality, Capote creates nightmares of the character's own making. It is up to the reader to determine what is real and what is not.

"Miriam" (continued) by Truman Capote

←—*Response notes*—→

Mrs. Miller spent the next day in bed, rising once to feed the canary and drink a cup of tea; she took her temperature and had none, yet her dreams were feverishly agitated; their unbalanced mood lingered even as she lay staring wide-eyed at the ceiling. One dream threaded through the others like an elusively mysterious theme in a complicated symphony, and the scenes it depicted were sharply outlined, as though sketched by a hand of gifted intensity: a small girl, wearing a bridal gown and a wreath of leaves, led a gray procession down a mountain path, and among them there was unusual silence till a woman at the rear asked, "Where is she taking us?" "No one knows," said an old man marching in front. "But isn't she pretty?" volunteered a third voice. "Isn't she like a frost flower . . . so shining and white?"

Tuesday morning she woke up feeling better; harsh slats of sunlight, slanting through Venetian blinds, shed a disrupting light on her unwholesome fancies. She opened the window to discover a thawed, mild-as-spring day; a sweep of clean new clouds crumpled against a vastly blue, out-of-season sky; and across the low line of rooftops she could see the river and smoke curving from tugboat stacks in a warm wind. A great silver truck plowed the snow-banked street, its machine sound humming on the air.

After straightening the apartment, she went to the grocer's, cashed a check and continued to Schrafft's, where she ate breakfast and chatted happily with the waitress. Oh, it was a wonderful day—more like a holiday—and it would be so foolish to go home.

She boarded a Lexington Avenue bus and rode up to Eighty-sixth Street; it was here that she had decided to do a little shopping.

She had no idea what she wanted or needed, but she idled along, intent only upon the passers-by, brisk and preoccupied, who gave her a disturbing sense of separateness.

It was while waiting at the corner of Third Avenue that she saw the man: an old man, bowlegged and stooped under an armload of bulging packages; he wore a shabby brown coat and a checkered cap. Suddenly she realized they were exchanging a smile: there was nothing friendly about this smile, it was merely two cold flickers of recognition. But she was certain she had never seen him before.

He was standing next to an El pillar, and as she crossed the street he turned and followed. He kept quite close; from the corner of her eye she watched his reflection wavering on the shopwindows.

Then in the middle of the block she stopped and faced him. He stopped also and cocked his head, grinning. But what could she say? Do? Here, in broad daylight, on Eighty-sixth Street? It was useless and, despising her own helplessness, she quickened her steps.

Now Second Avenue is a dismal street, made from scraps and ends; part cobblestone, part asphalt, part cement; and its atmosphere of desertion is permanent. Mrs. Miller walked five blocks without meeting anyone, and all the while the steady crunch of his footfalls in the snow stayed near. And when she came to a florist's shop, the sound was still with her. She hurried inside and watched through the glass door as the old man passed; he kept his eyes straight ahead and didn't slow his pace, but he did one strange, telling thing: he tipped his cap.

"Six white ones, did you say?" asked the florist. "Yes," she told him, "white roses." From there she went to a glassware store and selected a vase, presumably a replacement for the one Miriam had broken, though the price was intolerable and the vase itself (she thought) grotesquely vulgar. But a series of unaccountable purchases had begun, as if by prearranged plan: a plan of which she had not the least knowledge or control.

She bought a bag of glazed cherries, and at a place called the Knickerbocker Bakery she paid forty cents for six almond cakes.

Within the last hour the weather had turned cold again; like blurred lenses, winter clouds cast a shade over the sun, and the skeleton of an early dusk colored the sky; a damp mist mixed with the wind and the voices of a few children who romped high on mountains of gutter snow seemed lonely and cheerless. Soon the first flake fell, and when Mrs. Miller reached the brownstone house, snow was falling in a swift screen and foot tracks vanished as they were printed.

///// ///// ///// **STOP AND PREDICT** ///// /////

●◆ Review what you have read. Circle in the text the puzzling or mysterious events. Then describe what you think will happen next.

....

....

....

The white roses were arranged decoratively in the vase. The glazed cherries shone on a ceramic plate. The almond cakes, dusted with sugar, awaited a hand. The canary fluttered on its swing and picked at a bar of seed.

At precisely five the doorbell rang. Mrs. Miller knew who it was. The hem of her housecoat trailed as she crossed the floor. "Is that you?" she called.

"Miriam" by Truman Capote

←—Response notes—→

"Naturally," said Miriam, the word resounding shrilly from the hall. "Open this door."

"Go away," said Mrs. Miller.

"Please hurry . . . I have a heavy package."

"Go away," said Mrs. Miller. She returned to the living room, lighted a cigarette, sat down and calmly listened to the buzzer; on and on and on. "You might as well leave. I have no intention of letting you in."

Shortly the bell stopped. For possibly ten minutes Mrs. Miller did not move. Then, hearing no sound, she concluded Miriam had gone. She tiptoed to the door and opened it a sliver; Miriam was half-reclining atop a cardboard box with a beautiful French doll cradled in her arms.

"Really, I thought you were never coming," she said peevishly. "Here, help me get this in, it's awfully heavy."

It was not spell-like compulsion that Mrs. Miller felt, but rather a curious passivity; she brought in the box, Miriam, the doll. Miriam curled up on the sofa, not troubling to remove her coat or beret, and watched disinterestedly as Mrs. Miller dropped the box and stood trembling, trying to catch her breath.

"Thank you," she said. In the daylight she looked pinched and drawn, her hair less luminous. The French doll she was loving wore an exquisite powdered wig and its idiot glass eyes sought solace in Miriam's. "I have a surprise," she continued. "Look into my box."

Kneeling, Mrs. Miller parted the flaps and lifted out another doll; then a blue dress which she recalled as the one Miriam had worn that first night at the theater; and of the remainder she said, "It's all clothes. Why?"

"Because I've come to live with you," said Miriam, twisting a cherry stem. "Wasn't it nice of you to buy me the cherries . . . ?"

"But you can't! For God's sake go away—go away and leave me alone!"

". . . and the roses and the almond cakes? How really wonderfully generous. You know, these cherries are delicious. The last place I lived was with an old man; he was terribly poor and we never had good things to eat. But I think I'll be happy here." She paused to snuggle her doll closer. Now, if you'll just show me where to put my things . . ."

Mrs. Miller's face dissolved into a mask of ugly red lines; she began to cry, and it was an unnatural, tearless sort of weeping, as though, not having wept for a long time, she had forgotten how. Carefully she edged backward till she touched the door.

She fumbled through the hall and down the stairs to a landing below. She pounded frantically on the door of the first apartment she came to; a short, redheaded man answered and she pushed past him. "Say, what the hell is this?" he said. "Anything wrong, lover?" asked a young woman who appeared from the kitchen, drying her hands. And it was to her that Mrs. Miller turned.

"Listen," she cried, "I'm ashamed behaving this way but—well, I'm Mrs. H. T. Miller and I live upstairs and . . ." She pressed her hands

←—Response notes —→ over her face. "It sounds so absurd. . . ."

The woman guided her to a chair, while the man excitedly rattled pocket change. "Yeah?"

"I live upstairs and there's a little girl visiting me, and I suppose that I'm afraid of her. She won't leave and I can't make her and—she's going to do something terrible. She's already stolen my cameo, but she's about to do something worse—something terrible!"

The man asked, "Is she a relative, huh?"

Mrs. Miller shook her head. "I don't know who she is. Her name's Miriam, but I don't know for certain who she is."

"You gotta calm down, honey," said the woman, stroking Mrs. Miller's arm. "Harry here'll tend to this kid. Go on, lover." And Mrs. Miller said, "The door's open—5A."

After the man left, the woman brought a towel and bathed Mrs. Miller's face. "You're very kind," Mrs. Miller said. "I'm sorry to act like such a fool, only this wicked child . . ."

"Sure, honey," consoled the woman. "Now, you better take it easy."

Mrs. Miller rested her head in the crook of her arm; she was quiet enough to be asleep. The woman turned a radio dial; a piano and a husky voice filled the silence and the woman, tapping her foot, kept excellent time. "Maybe we oughta go up too," she said.

"I don't want to see her again. I don't want to be anywhere near her."

"Uh huh, but what you shoulda done, you shoulda called a cop."

Presently they heard the man on the stairs. He strode into the room frowning and scratching the back of his neck. "Nobody there," he said, honestly embarrassed. "She musta beat it."

"Harry, you're a jerk," announced the woman. "We been sitting here the whole time and we woulda seen . . ." she stopped abruptly, for the man's glance was sharp.

"I looked all over," he said, "and there just ain't nobody there. Nobody, understand?"

"Tell me," said Mrs. Miller, rising, "tell me, did you see a large box? Or a doll?"

"No, ma'am, I didn't."

And the woman, as if delivering a verdict, said, "Well, for cryinoutloud. . . ."

Mrs. Miller entered her apartment softly; she walked to the center of the room and stood quite still. No, in a sense it had not changed: the roses, the cakes, and the cherries were in place. But this was an empty room, emptier than if the furnishings and familiars were not present, lifeless and petrified as a funeral parlor. The sofa loomed before her with a new strangeness: its vacancy had a meaning that would have been less penetrating and terrible had Miriam been curled on it. She gazed fixedly at the space where she remembered setting the box and, for a moment, the hassock spun desperately. And she looked through the window; surely the river was real, surely snow was falling—but then, one could not be certain witness to anything: Miriam, so vividly there—and yet, where was she? Where, where?

"Miriam" by Truman Capote

As though moving in a dream, she sank to a chair. The room was losing shape; it was dark and getting darker and there was nothing to be done about it; she could not lift her hand to light a lamp.

Suddenly, closing her eyes, she felt an upward surge, like a diver emerging from some deeper, greener depth. In times of terror or immense distress, there are moments when the mind waits, as though for a revelation, while a skein of calm is woven over thought; it is like a sleep, or a supernatural trance; and during this lull one is aware of a force of quiet reasoning: well, what if she had never really known a girl named Miriam? that she had been foolishly frightened on the street? In the end, like everything else, it was of no importance. For the only thing she had lost to Miriam was her identity, but now she knew she had found again the person who lived in this room, who cooked her own meals, who owned a canary, who was someone she could trust and believe in: Mrs. H. T. Miller.

Listening in contentment, she became aware of a double sound: a bureau drawer opening and closing; she seemed to hear it long after completion—opening and closing. Then gradually, the harshness of it was replaced by the murmur of a silk dress and this, delicately faint, was moving nearer and swelling in intensity till the walls trembled with the vibration and the room was caving under a wave of whispers. Mrs. Miller stiffened and opened her eyes to a dull, direct stare.

"Hello," said Miriam.

←——Response notes——→

107

What is real in this story? Who is Miriam? Some readers have suggested that she is Mrs. Miller's repressed self or that she is a hallucination. In the chart below, list details that indicate Miriam is real in the left column and details that indicate she is a hallucination in the right.

real	hallucination

●◆ Write a letter to a friend who has also read this story. In your letter, tell your friend what you think about Mrs. Miller. Go back over the story to gather evidence for your interpretation of her behavior and personality. Then, support your interpretation with quotations from the text.

Readers must form and support their interpretations of a story after carefully considering the details

Five Reading Literary Criticism

The poet James Dickey delivered a speech about Truman Capote at the annual meeting of the American Academy and Institute of Arts and Letters. In it he focused on Capote's talent as a writer. Think about what Dickey's words add to your idea of Capote from "Louis Armstrong" and "Miriam."

from a Speech by James Dickey

← *Response notes* →

I find myself returning often to *Other Voices, Other Rooms*, but more often to the shorter pieces of *The Tree of Night*, and I believe I do this because I think of Capote's gift as essentially lyrical, poetic: the stamp-minted event, the scene stunning with rightness and strangeness, the compressed phrase, the exact yet imaginative word, the devastating metaphorical aptness, a feeling of concentrated excess which at the same time gives the effect of being crystalline. One can say of these stories, like "Miriam" and "Shut a Final Door," which in other hands would bear too many resemblances to gothic movies, with lots of melodrama, props, grotesque stage businesses, that they are saved by the only quality that can save any writer's anything: his personal vision, which in Capote's case runs to unforgettable images of fear, hopelessness, and dream-death: in addition to cold, also its opposite: aimlessness, heat, ripe rot, the submerged corpse green in the moveless pool.

It is maybe paradoxical, but not finally so, that such images—many of his best—of the stultified, the still, the overhot and overripe come like the others from Truman Capote's lenslike detachment, and suggest, rather than lushness and softness, things wrought by the engraver's delicate hammer, the artist working with otherworldly intensity upon materials from the world, as the universe makes a snowflake, the most fastidiously created of artifacts, resulting in a true work of literature, which, unlike the snowflake, keeps on existing. The sure-handed crystal-making detachment, the integrity of concentration, the craft of the artist by means of which the intently human thing is caught, Truman Capote had, and not just at certain times but at all times. This we remember, and will keep, for it gave us what of him will stay. Keep him we will, and from such a belief come these few lines, something.

109

In the first paragraph of this excerpt, Dickey lists several elements of Capote's **style**. Dickey helps us see aspects of Capote's work that we might not otherwise. Yet, his view needs to be validated by rereading Capote's work. In the chart on the next page, cite examples from the two works you have read that illustrate some of the phrases Dickey uses.

Dickey's description	Example from Capote
"lyrical, poetic"	
"compressed phrase"	
"unforgettable images of fear"	
"the stultified, the still, the overhot and overripe" images	

●◆ Now write an analysis of Dickey's points. Do you agree or disagree with what he wrote about Capote?

Literary critics can sometimes help readers see new aspects of an author's work.

Essentials of Reading

What are the essentials of reading? good light? a comfortable chair? no distractions? All true, but they will not help you understand what you read. There are also essentials for reading actively.

Predicting as you read will help you access your previous knowledge. Analyzing the imagery and word choice will help you determine the tone of a piece. Making inferences will help you move beyond simple comprehension. Focusing on the theme will help you figure out what the author is saying. And, thinking about the tone will help you understand the author's purpose in writing. In this unit, you are going to focus on these five strategies. They can increase your understanding and enjoyment of reading.

These five strategies can help you become a more active—and interested—reader, and help you learn more from what you read.

One Thinking With the Writer

Each time you pause in the middle of reading and ask yourself, "What's going to happen?" you make a prediction about the outcome of the story. Predictions are an essential part of reading because, as you predict, you are using your previous knowledge to understand something new. Predicting enables you to read actively.

As you read this short story by Jerome Weidman, make some predictions about what will happen.

"My Father Sits in the Dark" by Jerome Weidman

← Response notes →

My father has a peculiar habit. He is fond of sitting in the dark, alone. Sometimes I come home very late. The house is dark. I let myself in quietly because I do not want to disturb my mother. She is a light sleeper. I tiptoe into my room and undress in the dark. I go to the kitchen for a drink of water. My bare feet make no noise. I step into the room and almost trip over my father. He is sitting in a kitchen chair, in his pajamas, smoking his pipe.

"Hello, Pop," I say.

"Hello, son."

"Why don't you go to bed, Pa?"

"I will," he says.

But he remains there. Long after I am asleep I feel sure that he is still sitting there, smoking.

Many times I am reading in my room. I hear my mother get the house ready for the night. I hear my kid brother go to bed. I hear my sister come in. I hear her do things with jars and combs until she, too, is quiet. I know she has gone to sleep. In a little while I hear my mother say good night to my father. I continue to read. Soon I become thirsty. (I drink a lot of water.) I go to the kitchen for a drink. Again I almost stumble across my father. Many times it startles me. I forget about him. And there he is—smoking, sitting, thinking.

"Why don't you go to bed, Pop?"

"I will, son."

But he doesn't. He just sits there and smokes and thinks. It worries me. I can't understand it. What can he be thinking about? Once I asked him.

"What are you thinking about, Pa?"

"Nothing," he said.

Once I left him there and went to bed. I awoke several hours later. I was thirsty. I went to the kitchen. There he was. His pipe was out. But he sat there, staring into a corner of the kitchen. After a moment I became accustomed to the darkness. I took my drink. He still sat and stared. His eyes did not blink. I thought he was not even aware of me. I was afraid.

"Why don't you go to bed, Pop?"

"I will, son," he said. "Don't wait up for me."

"But," I said, "you've been sitting here for hours. What's wrong? What are you thinking about?"

"Nothing, son," he said. "Nothing. It's just restful. That's all."

The way he said it was convincing. He did not seem worried. His

"My Father Sits in the Dark" by Jerome Weidman

voice was even and pleasant. It always is. But I could not understand
it. How could it be restful to sit alone in an uncomfortable chair far
into the night, in darkness?

What can it be?

STOP AND PREDICT

➽ Why does the father sit in the kitchen in the dark?

I review all the possibilities. It can't be money. I know that. We
haven't much, but when he is worried about money he makes no
secret of it. It can't be his health. He is not reticent about that either.
It can't be the health of anyone in the family. We are a bit short on
money, but we are long on health. (Knock wood, my mother would
say.) What can it be? I am afraid I do not know. But that does not
stop me from worrying.

Maybe he is thinking of his brothers in the old country. Or of his
mother and two step-mothers. Or of his father. But they are all dead.
And he would not brood about them like that. I say brood, but it is not
really true. He does not brood. He does not even seem to be thinking.
He looks too peaceful, too, well not contented, just too peaceful, to be
brooding. Perhaps it is as he says. Perhaps it is restful. But it does
not seem possible. It worries me.

If I only knew what he thinks about. If I only knew what he thinks
at all. I might not be able to help him. He might not even need help. It
may be as he says. It may be restful. But at least I would not worry
about it.

Why does he just sit there, in the dark? Is his mind failing? No, it
can't be. He is only fifty-three. And he is just as keen-witted as ever.
In fact, he is the same in every respect. He still likes beet soup. He
still reads the second section of the *Times* first. He still wears wing
collars. He still believes that the Debs could have saved the country
and that T. R. was a tool of the moneyed interest. He is the same in
every way. He does not even look older than he did five years ago.
Everybody remarks about that. Well-preserved, they say. But he sits
in the dark, alone, smoking, staring straight ahead of him, unblinking,
into the small hours of the night.

If it is as he says, if it is restful, I will let it go at that. But
suppose it is not. Suppose it is something I cannot fathom. Perhaps he
needs help. Why doesn't he speak? Why doesn't he frown or laugh or
cry? Why doesn't he do something? Why does he just sit there?

Finally I become angry. Maybe it is just my unsatisfied curiosity.
Maybe I *am* a bit worried. Anyway, I become angry.

"Is something wrong, Pop?"

"Nothing, son. Nothing at all."

But this time I am determined not to be put off. I am angry.

"Then why do you sit here all alone, thinking, till late?"

"My Father Sits in the Dark" by Jerome Weidman

← Response notes →

"It's restful, son. I like it."

I am getting nowhere. Tomorrow he will be sitting there again. I will be puzzled. I will be worried. I will not stop now. I am angry.

"Well, what do you *think* about, Pa? Why do you just sit here? What's worrying you? What do you think about?"

"Nothing's worrying me, son. I'm all right. It's just restful. That's all. Go to bed, son."

My anger has left me. But the feeling of worry is still there. I must get an answer. It seems so silly. Why doesn't he tell me? I have a funny feeling that unless I get an answer, I will go crazy. I am insistent.

"But what do you *think* about, Pa? What is it?"

"Nothing, son. Just things in general. Nothing special. Just things."

I can get no answer.

It is very late. The street is quiet and the house is dark. I climb the steps softly, skipping the ones that creak. I let myself in with my key and tiptoe into my room. I remove my clothes and remember that I am thirsty. In my bare feet I walk to the kitchen. Before I reach it I know he is there.

STOP AND PREDICT

What will the son do? Will he confront his father?

114

I can see the deeper darkness of his hunched shape. He is sitting in the same chair, his elbows on his knees, his cold pipe in his teeth, his unblinking eyes staring straight ahead. He does not seem to know I am there. He did not hear me come in. I stand quietly in the doorway and watch him.

Everything is quiet, but the night is full of little sounds. As I stand there motionless I begin to notice them. The ticking of the alarm clock on the icebox. The low hum of an automobile passing many blocks away. The swish of papers moved along the street by the breeze. A whispering rise and fall of sound, like low breathing. It is strangely pleasant.

The dryness in my throat reminds me. I step briskly into the kitchen.

"Hello, Pop," I say.

"Hello, son," he says. His voice is low and dreamlike. He does not change his position or shift his gaze.

I cannot find the faucet. The dim shadow of light that comes through the window from the street only makes the room seem darker. I reach for the short chain in the center of the room. I snap on the light.

He straightens up with a jerk, as though he has been struck. "What's the matter, Pop?" I ask.

"Nothing," he says. "I don't like the light."

"What's the matter with the light?" I say. "What's wrong?"

"My Father Sits in the Dark" by Jerome Weidman

"Nothing, he says. "I don't like the light."

I snap the light off. I drink my water slowly. I must take it easy, I say to myself. I must get to the bottom of this.

"Why don't you go to bed? Why do you sit here so late in the dark?"

← Response notes →

STOP AND PREDICT

●◆ What do you think the father will answer?

....

....

"It's nice," he says. "I can't get used to lights. We didn't have lights when I was a boy in Europe."

My heart skips a beat and I catch my breath happily. I begin to think I understand. I remember the stories of his boyhood in Austria. I see the wide-beamed *kretchma,* with my grandfather behind the bar. It is late, the customers are gone, and he is dozing. I see the bed of glowing coals, the last of the roaring fire. The room is already dark, and growing darker. I see a small boy, crouched on a pile of twigs at one side of the huge fireplace, his starry gaze fixed on the dull remains of the dead flames. The boy is my father.

I remember the pleasure of those few moments when I stood quietly in the doorway watching him.

"You mean there's nothing wrong? You just sit in the dark because you like it, Pop?" I find it hard to keep my voice from rising in a happy shout.

"Sure," he says. "I can't think with the light on."

I set my glass down and turn to go back to my room. "Good night, Pop," I say.

"Good night," he says.

Then I remember. I turn back. "What do you think about, Pop?" I ask.

His voice seems to come from far away. It is quiet and even again. "Nothing," he says softly. "Nothing special."

●◆ How would you describe the father in the story? Weidman offers very little description of him. Reread the story and then write a short description of the father.

....

....

....

....

....

115

●◆ Write a letter from the father to a friend describing his son's worries. Inhabit the father's character to try and explain his preference for thinking in the dark and also his trouble explaining it to his son.

116

Two Analyzing Tone

Tone is the writer's attitude toward a subject. It is conveyed to the reader by a combination of **rhythm**, word choice, and **imagery**. Understanding the **tone** is one of the keys to figuring out the **theme** and purpose of a work of literature.

Read this passage from *Cold Mountain*, a novel by Charles Frazier. As you read, circle or highlight things in the text that contribute to the tone.

from *Cold Mountain* by Charles Frazier

← *Response notes* →

At the first gesture of morning, flies began stirring. Inman's eyes and the long wound at his neck drew them, and the sound of their wings and the touch of their feet were soon more potent than a yardful of roosters in rousing a man to wake. So he came to yet one more day in the hospital ward. He flapped the flies away with his hands and looked across the foot of his bed to an open triple-hung window. Ordinarily he could see to the red road and the oak tree and the low brick wall. And beyond them to a sweep of fields and flat piney woods that stretched to the western horizon. The view was a long one for the flatlands, the hospital having been built on the only swell within eyeshot. But it was too early yet for a vista. The window might as well have been painted grey.

Had it not been too dim, Inman would have read to pass the time until breakfast, for the book he was reading had the effect of settling his mind. But he had burned up the last of his own candles reading to bring sleep the night before, and lamp oil was too scarce to be striking the hospital's lights for mere diversion. So he rose and dressed and sat in a ladderback chair, putting the gloomy room of beds and their broken occupants behind him. He flapped again at the flies and looked out the window at the first smear of foggy dawn and waited for the world to begin shaping up outside.

The window was tall as a door, and he had imagined many times that it would open onto some other place and let him walk through and be there. During his first weeks in the hospital, he had been hardly able to move his head, and all that kept his mind occupied had been watching out the window and picturing the old green places he recollected from home. Childhood places. The damp creek bank where Indian pipes grew. The corner of a meadow favored by brown-and-black caterpillars in the fall. A hickory limb that overhung the lane, and from which he often watched his father driving cows down to the barn at dusk. They would pass underneath him, and then he would close his eyes and listen as the cupping sound of their hooves in the dirt grew fainter and fainter until it vanished into the calls of katy-dids and peepers. The window apparently wanted only to take his thoughts back. Which was fine with him, for he had seen the metal face of the age and had been so stunned by it that when he thought into the future, all he could vision was a world from which everything he counted important had been banished or had willingly fled.

117

Reading aloud is an excellent way to focus on the tone of a text. Listen while someone reads the excerpt aloud.

●◆ Describe the tone of this piece.

●◆ Go back and reread "My Father Sits in the Dark." What is the tone of the story?

●◆ Compare the way the tone works in the two pieces. How are your impressions of the characters (the son, the father, and Inman) affected by the tone?

Tone
is the overall feeling or
effect created by a writer's use
of words, imagery, and
rhythm.

Three
Reading Between the Lines

Critical readers know how important it is to make **inferences** while reading. Inferences are the reasonable conclusions a reader can make using the details provided in a story. The author describes how the characters look, act, and talk, and then leaves it to the reader to infer what they are really like.

As you read "The End of Something" by Ernest Hemingway, note your impressions of the two main characters, Nick and Marjorie.

"The End of Something" by Ernest Hemingway

← *Response notes* →

In the old days Hortons Bay was a lumbering town. No one who lived in it was out of sound of the big saws in the mill by the lake. Then one year there were no more logs to make lumber. The lumber schooners came into the bay and were loaded with the cut of the mill that stood stacked in the yard. All the piles of lumber were carried away. The big mill building had all its machinery that was removable taken out and hoisted on board one of the schooners by the men who had worked in the mill. The schooner moved out of the bay toward the open lake, carrying the two great saws, the traveling carriage that hurled the logs against the revolving, circular saws and all the rollers, wheels, belts and iron piled on a hulldeep load of lumber. Its open hold covered with canvas and lashed tight, the sails of the schooner filled and it moved out into the open lake, carrying with it everything that had made the mill a mill and Hortons Bay a town.

The one-story bunkhouses, the eating house, the company store, the mill offices, and the big mill itself stood deserted in the acres of sawdust that covered the swampy meadow by the shore of the bay.

Ten years later there was nothing of the mill left except the broken white limestone of its foundations showing through the swampy second growth as Nick and Marjorie rowed along the shore. They were trolling along the edge of the channel bank where the bottom dropped off suddenly from sandy shallows to twelve feet of dark water. They were trolling on their way to the point to set night lines for rainbow trout.

"There's our old ruin, Nick," Marjorie said.

Nick, rowing, looked at the white stone in the green trees.

"There it is," he said.

"Can you remember when it was a mill?" Marjorie asked.

"I can just remember," Nick said.

"It seems more like a castle," Marjorie said.

Nick said nothing. They rowed on out of sight of the mill, following the shore line. Then Nick cut across the bay.

"They aren't striking," he said.

"No," Marjorie said. She was intent on the rod all the time they trolled, even when she talked. She loved to fish. She loved to fish with Nick.

Close beside the boat a big trout broke the surface of the water. Nick pulled hard on one oar so the boat would turn and the bait,

119

spinning far behind, would pass where the trout was feeding. As the trout's back came up out of the water the minnows jumped wildly. They sprinkled the surface like a handful of shot thrown into the water. Another trout broke water, feeding on the other side of the boat.

"They're feeding," Marjorie said.

"But they won't strike," Nick said.

He rowed the boat around to troll past both the feeding fish, then headed it for the point. Marjorie did not reel in until the boat touched the shore.

They pulled the boat up the beach and Nick lifted out a pail of live perch. The perch swam in the water pail. Nick caught three of them with his hands and cut their heads off and skinned them while Marjorie chased with her hands in the bucket, finally caught a perch, cut its head off and skinned it. Nick looked at her fish.

"You don't want to take the ventral fin out," he said. "It'll be all right for bait but it's better with the ventral fin in."

He hooked each of the skinned perch through the tail. There were two hooks attached to a leader on each rod. Then Marjorie rowed the boat out over the channel-bank, holding the line in her teeth, and looking toward Nick, who stood on the shore holding the rod and letting the line run out from the reel.

"That's about right," he called.

"Should I let it drop?" Marjorie called back, holding the line in her hand.

"Sure. Let it go." Marjorie dropped the line overboard and watched the baits go down through the water.

She came in with the boat and ran the second line out the same way. Each time Nick set a heavy slab of driftwood across the butt of the rod to hold it solid and propped it up at an angle with a small slab. He reeled in the slack line so the line ran taut out to where the bait rested on the sandy floor of the channel and set the click on the reel. When a trout, feeding on the bottom, took the bait it would run with it, taking line out of the reel in a rush and making the reel sing with the click on.

Marjorie rowed up the point a little way so she would not disturb the line. She pulled hard on the oars and the boat went up the beach. Little waves came in with it. Marjorie stepped out of the boat and Nick pulled the boat high up the beach.

"What's the matter, Nick?" Marjorie asked.

"I don't know," Nick said, getting wood for a fire.

They made a fire with driftwood. Marjorie went to the boat and brought a blanket. The evening breeze blew the smoke toward the point, so Marjorie spread the blanket out between the fire and the lake.

Marjorie sat on the blanket with her back to the fire and waited for Nick. He came over and sat down beside her on the blanket. In back of them was the close second-growth timber of the point and in front was the bay with the mouth of Hortons Creek. It was not quite

120

dark. The firelight went as far as the water. They could both see the two steel rods at an angle over the dark water. The fire glinted on the reels.

Marjorie unpacked the basket of supper.

"I don't feel like eating," said Nick.

"Come on and eat, Nick."

"All right."

They ate without talking and watched the two rods and the firelight in the water.

"There's going to be a moon tonight," said Nick. He looked across the bay to the hills that were beginning to sharpen against the sky. Beyond the hills he knew the moon was coming up.

"I know it," Marjorie said happily.

"You know everything," Nick said.

"Oh, Nick, please cut it out! Please, please don't be that way!"

"I can't help it," Nick said. "You do. You know everything. That's the trouble. You know you do."

Marjorie did not say anything.

"I've taught you everything. You know you do. What don't you know, anyway?"

"Oh shut up," Marjorie said. "There comes the moon."

They sat on the blanket without touching each other and watched the moon rise.

"You don't have to talk silly," Marjorie said. "What's really the matter?"

"I don't know."

"Of course you know."

"No I don't"

"Go on and say it."

Nick looked on at the moon, coming up over the hills.

"It isn't fun any more."

He was afraid to look at Marjorie. Then he looked at her. She sat there with her back toward him. He looked at her back. "It isn't fun any more. Not any of it."

She didn't say anything. He went on. "I feel as though everything has gone to hell inside of me. I don't know, Marge. I don't know what to say."

He looked on at her back.

"Isn't love any fun?" Marjorie said.

"No," Nick said. Marjorie stood up. Nick sat there, his head in his hands.

"I'm going to take the boat," Marjorie called to him. "You can walk back around the point."

"All right," Nick said. "I'll push the boat off for you."

"You don't need to," she said. She was afloat in the boat on the water with the moonlight on it. Nick went back and lay down with his face in the blanket by the fire. He could hear Marjorie rowing on the water.

He lay there for a long time. He lay there while he heard Bill come into the clearing, walking around the woods. He felt Bill coming up to

"The End of Something" by Ernest Hemingway

←—Response notes—→ the fire. Bill didn't touch him, either.

"Did she go all right?" Bill said.

"Oh, yes," Nick said, lying, his face on the blanket.

"Have a scene?"

"No, there wasn't any scene."

"How do you feel?"

"Oh, go away, Bill! Go away for a while." Bill selected a sandwich from the lunch basket and walked over to have a look at the rods.

●◆ What can you infer about the characters? Use the chart below to describe Nick and Marjorie. List phrases or sentences in the left column. In the right column, note what you inferred about the characters.

Quotation	What I can infer about Nick or Marjorie
"It seems more like a castle," Marjorie said.	Marjorie's more romantic than Nick

122

➡◆Imagine you are Marjorie's friend. What advice do you want to give her about Nick? Should she give him another chance? Write a note to Marjorie advising her what to do. Use comments from the inference chart to help you give her advice.

Critical readers know that making inferences about a story's characters will improve their understanding of the work as a whole.

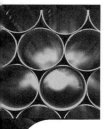

Four Thinking Theme

Every kind of writing—fiction, nonfiction, or poetry—has a **theme**. It is the generalization about life, people, or ideas that the author wants to make. A theme may be stated directly, but it is more often implied. A story, novel, or poem that is particularly rich or complex may have several themes. Not every reader will make the same **inferences** about a work's themes.

Reread "The End of Something" and review your response notes.

• **What does Hemingway spend the most time talking about or describing?**

• **What is Hemingway's attitude toward the thing he describes?**

• **Summarize the story in one sentence.**

124

➥ Use the cluster below to note the themes of "The End of Something."

Themes in
"The End of
Something"

> If you can understand the story's theme, you can identify and understand the message the author has for you.

When you finish your cluster, return to Hemingway's story. Underline the words, sentences, and paragraphs that relate to the themes you identified.

Five Author's Purpose

Most of the time an author does not come right out and make a statement about his or her purpose. Instead, the author trusts the reader will make **inferences** about the meaning of the story. Critical readers know that the author's **tone** is a valuable clue. If, for example, you know that the tone of a piece of writing is sarcastic, you might infer that the writer's intent is to mock someone or something. If the tone of a piece is humorous, you might assume that the primary intent is to entertain.

In the following excerpt from his memoir, *Notes of a Native Son,* James Baldwin recalls his father. What does Baldwin's tone reveal about his purpose?

from *Notes of a Native Son* by James Baldwin

←Response notes→

He was, I think, very handsome. I gather this from photographs and from my own memories of him, dressed in his Sunday best and on his way to preach a sermon somewhere, when I was little. Handsome, proud, and ingrown, "like a toenail," somebody said. But he looked to me, as I grew older, like pictures I had seen of African tribal chieftains: he really should have been naked, with warpaint on and barbaric mementos, standing among spears. He could be chilling in the pulpit and indescribably cruel in his personal life and he was certainly the most bitter man I have ever met; yet it must be said that there was something else in him, buried in him, which lent him his tremendous power and, even, a rather crushing charm. It had to do with his blackness, I think—he was very black—with his blackness and his beauty, and with the fact that he knew that he was black but did not know that he was beautiful. He claimed to be proud of his blackness but it had also been the cause of much humiliation and it had fixed bleak boundaries to his life. He was not a young man when we were growing up and he had already suffered many kinds of ruin; in his outrageously demanding and protective way he loved his children, who were black like him and menaced, like him; and all these things sometimes showed in his face when he tried, never to my knowledge with any success, to establish contact with any of us. When he took one of his children on his knee to play, the child always became fretful and began to cry; when he tried to help one of us with our homework the absolutely unabating tension which emanated from him caused our minds and our tongues to become paralyzed, so that he, scarcely knowing why, flew into a rage and the child, not knowing why, was punished. If it ever entered his head to bring a surprise home for his children, it was, almost unfailingly, the wrong surprise and even the big watermelons he often brought home on his back in the summertime led to the most appalling scenes. I do not remember, in all those years, that one of his children was ever glad to see him come home.

Notice the slow, deliberate, "I'm-thinking-things-through" tone of Baldwin's piece. He appears to be writing down his memories as they occur to him and makes it clear to the reader that he will not try to soften or change his memories in order to paint a more flattering picture of his father.

125

●◆ How would you describe the tone of Baldwin's writing?

....

....

....

....

●◆ What words and images create the tone?

....

....

....

....

●◆ What is Baldwin's purpose in this piece about his father? Describe his intention and how the tone helps you determine it.

....

....

....

....

....

....

....

....

....

....

....

An important first step in understanding the author's intent is understanding the tone of the writing.

History Through Story

Stories are often told about historical events. The motivation for writing these stories varies—to remember important moments, to share the personal or public meaning of the events, or to raise questions about future actions. For example, the internment of 100,000 Japanese Americans in the United States during World War II has compelled many people to write. Executive Order 9066 set into motion the mass evacuation and imprisonment of Japanese Americans in the United States in 1942. Two-thirds of the internees were citizens, a fact quickly forgotten in the hysteria after the bombing of Pearl Harbor. Men, women, and children of Japanese ancestry were uprooted from their homes and sent to makeshift camps in the supposed interest of national security. They were finally released in 1944 when the Supreme Court ruled it unconstitutional to imprison law-abiding citizens. For decades, the Japanese American story of incarceration was largely kept quiet. As Harry Kawahara wrote, "Our self-esteem, our self-regard, was shattered. We did not feel comfortable talking about our camp experience with others." The stories that have grown out of the silence give us a chance to examine this event.

One Personal Narratives

Personal **narratives** offer readers the chance to learn firsthand about important events. Few *Issei* (immigrants from Japan) told their stories about the internment, but many *Nisei* (the children of the *issei*) Japanese Americans have written about the experience. Yoshiko Uchida was five months from graduating from the University of California at Berkeley when Japan bombed Pearl Harbor on December 7, 1941. Uchida did not graduate that next summer; she was interned and spent the next several years in camps. In an excerpt from her **autobiography**, Uchida describes the train ride from a makeshift camp in California to a more permanent one in Utah.

from *The Invisible Thread* by Yoshiko Uchida

←—Response notes—→

By noon the next day we were in Nevada sagebrush country. Suddenly, in the middle of an absolutely desolate stretch of desert, the train pulled to a stop. Our car captain announced that we could all get off for a thirty-minute break to stretch our legs.

"But don't go beyond the row of MPs," he warned.

Or what, I wondered. Would they shoot?

I saw the row of helmeted MPs lined up between our train and the desert, and wondered who would want to escape in this godforsaken patch of land. All any of us wanted was to stretch our sore muscles and breathe a little fresh air.

By the second night on the train, we were all so stiff and numb, sleep was out of the question. I could hardly wait to get to Utah.

About 9:30 P.M. we crossed the Great Salt Lake, and the car captain turned out the lights and allowed us to raise the blinds so we could look out.

I caught my breath at the sight of the magnificent lake shimmering in the moonlight. It looked so serene and majestic—a part of something so much greater than our small rickety prison train. It was as though we'd been given a few magical moments from the earth, as a gift, to carry in our hearts into the concentration camp.

When we reached the Salt Lake City station, we quickly opened the windows to catch a glimpse of the "real world." It felt good to hear the busy normal sounds of the station and the calls of the men who were servicing our train.

As I thrust my head out of the window to take it all in, I was astonished to see a familiar face. It was one of my former Nisei classmates from the university.

"Helen! What in the world are you doing here?" I asked.

She told me she had evacuated voluntarily, moving out of the restricted zone before the uprooting, and was now living in Salt Lake City. "When I heard the internee train was coming through," she explained, "I came to see if I could find anybody I knew."

from *The Invisible Thread* by Yoshiko Uchida

←—Response notes—→

She was anxious to know what had happened to other friends in our class.

"They're scattered everywhere," I told her, "in camps all over the United States."

We talked as fast as we could, exchanging news of what had happened to each of us since we last spoke on campus. And then it was time for the train to leave. She took my hand briefly.

"Good luck, Yo."

"Thanks," I said, "I think I'll need it."

I waved to her as the train slowly pulled out of the station, thinking how lucky she was. She was free to return to her own home and live like a normal person. But I was still a prisoner, simply because I had not been able to evacuate voluntarily as she had. It didn't make sense. I was filled with envy as I leaned back on the hard seat and tried to get some sleep.

We finally reached Delta, Utah, the next morning. I was so anxious to get off the train, I didn't even mind being counted again as we filed off. For the last leg of our journey to Topaz, we were transferred to buses.

The scenery outside looked encouraging, for I saw many small farms and cultivated fields.

"Maybe it won't be so bad out there," I said hopefully.

But Kay just said, "Don't get your hopes up too soon, Yo."

And she was right. We had only ridden for about a half hour when there was a sudden change of scenery. There were no more trees or fields or vegetation of any kind.

Soon all we could see were dry clumps of greasewood. We were entering the edge of the Sevier Desert fifteen miles east of Delta, and the surroundings now were as bleak as a bleached bone.

The bus made a sudden turn into the heart of the sun-drenched desert, and there, in the middle of nowhere, were rows and rows of tar-papered barracks. They looked like small match boxes laid out neatly on a vast white table.

This was Topaz, one of ten such concentration camps in which Japanese Americans were interned throughout the United States. All of them were in equally barren and isolated areas and were operated by a civilian agency called the War Relocation Authority.

129

Personal narratives are retellings of real experience. Writers tend to use the techniques of fiction in order to achieve dramatic effect. In much of her narrative, Uchida describes what happened in such a way that the details express her emotional reactions or opinions without her stating them.

Discuss with a partner how the details Uchida uses convey her feelings.

●◆ Write a personal narrative of your own that describes a time when you were in a difficult situation or felt like an outsider. Think of the story you want to tell. Describe in detail the setting where the incident took place. Let the details reveal your feelings and reactions to the incident.

130

Personal narratives are retellings of real events that carefully reconstruct the personal experience to reveal the author's reactions to them and their significance.

Two

A Twice-Told Story

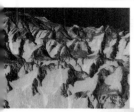

Jeanne Wakatsuki Houston was seven years old when her family was sent to live in an internment camp in California. She spent the next three-and-a-half years of her life at Manzanar. Writing *Farewell to Manzanar* was a way, she wrote, "of coming to terms with the impact these years have had on my entire life." In one of her last chapters, Houston tells about her journey back to the camp thirty years after she lived there.

from ***Farewell to Manzanar*** by Jeanne Wakatsuki Houston

←—— Response notes ——→

It was April 1972, thirty years almost to the day, that we piled our three kids into the car and headed out there. From where we live now, in the California coast town of Santa Cruz, it's a full day's drive. We started down 101 to Paso Robles, crossed over the hummocky Diablo range to the central valley, skirted Bakersfield, and climbed through Tehachpi Pass into the desert.

At Mojave we turned north onto the same road our bus had taken out from Los Angeles in April 1942. It is the back road to the Sierras and the main route from southern California to Reno and Lake Tahoe. We joined bikers and backpackers and the skiers heading for Mammoth. The traffic through there is fast, everyone but the bikers making for the high country. As we sped along wide roads at sixty and seventy, with our kids exclaiming at the sights we passed and our car loaded down with camping gear, it seemed even more incredible to me that a place like Manzanar could have been anywhere within reach of such a highway, such a caravan of pleasure-seeking travelers.

The bikers peeled off at Red Rock Canyon, a gorgeous bulge of pink cliffs and rusty gulches humping out of the flatlands. After that it was lovely desert but nothing much to stop for. In a hundred miles we passed two oases, the first at Olancha, the second around Lone Pine, a small, tree-filled town where a lot of mountain buffs turn off for the Mount Whitney Portal.

A few miles out of Lone Pine we started looking for another stand of trees, some tall elms, and what remains of those gnarled pear orchards. They were easy to spot. Everything else is sagebrush, tumbleweeds, and wind.

At its peak, in the summer of '42, Manzanar was the biggest city between Reno and Los Angeles, a special kind of western boom town that sprang from the sand, flourished, had its day, and now has all but disappeared. The barracks are gone, torn down right after the war. The guard towers are gone, and the mess halls and shower rooms, the hospital, the tea gardens, and the white buildings outside the compound. Even the dust is gone. Spreading brush holds it to the ground. Thirty years earlier, army bulldozers had scraped everything clean to start construction.

What you see from the road are the two gatehouses, each a small empty pillbox of a building faced with flagstones and topped, like tiny pagodas, with shingled curving roofs. Farther in, you see the elms, from **Farewell to Manzanar** by Jeanne Wakatsuki Houston

most of which were planted by internees, and off to the right a large green building that was once our high school auditorium, now a maintenance depot for the Los Angeles Power and Water District, who leased the land to the government during the war and still owns it.

Past the gatehouses we turned left over a cattle guard and onto a dirt perimeter road that led to the far side of the campsite. About half a mile in we spotted a white obelisk gleaming in the distance and marking a subtle line where the plain begins gradually to slope upward into the alluvial fan that becomes the base of the mountains. It seemed miraculous, as if some block of stone had fallen from the peaks above and landed upright in the brush, chiseled, solitary, twelve feet high.

Near it a dozen graves were outlined in the sand with small stones, and a barbed-wire fence surrounded them to keep back the cattle and the tumbleweed. The black Japanese script cut into the white face of the obelisk read simply, "A Memorial to the Dead."

We were alone out there, too far from the road to hear anything but wind. I thought of Mama, now seven years gone. For a long time I stood gazing at the monument. I couldn't step inside the fence. I believe in ghosts and spirits. I knew I was in the presence of those who had died at Manzanar. I also felt the spiritual presence that always lingers near awesome wonders like Mount Whitney. Then, as if rising from the ground around us on the valley floor, I began to hear the first whispers, nearly inaudible, from all those thousands who once had lived out here, a wide, windy sound of the ghost of that life. As we began to walk, it grew to a murmur, a thin steady hum.

132

The twice-told narrative is a story that reviews past events as it describes some present action. Reread the excerpt and highlight descriptions of the present in one color and descriptions of the past in another color.

● ● What is the main impression you take away from Houston's double telling? What effect does the blending of two different times have on you as a reader?

....

....

....

....

....

Discuss with a partner the similarities and differences in your reactions to the subject of Japanese internment as represented by Uchida and Houston. How are your reactions influenced by the different ways in which each of the stories is told? What do you see as the strengths or weaknesses of each?

Retell the incident you wrote in Lesson One as a twice-told story. If you have not actually gone back to the place where the incident occurred, take the journey in your mind. Keep in mind that you need to review the past incident as you are describing the place in the present.

133

Often writers present the past and present simultaneously in a personal narrative. It allows them to review the events of the past from a more objective perspective.

The stories about a historical event take many shapes and forms. Each offers a unique interpretation, partly because of the way the story gets told. In the following poem, Dwight Okita, a third-generation Japanese American, imagines his mother's reaction to the decision—Executive Order 9066—to intern all the Japanese Americans.

Response notes

In Response to Executive Order 9066
Dwight Okita

Dear Sirs:
    Of course I'll come. I've packed my galoshes
    and three packets of tomato seeds. Denise calls them
    love apples. My father says where we're going
    they won't grow.

    I am a fourteen-year-old girl with bad spelling
    and a messy room. If it helps any, I will tell you
    I have always felt funny using chopsticks
    and my favorite food is hot dogs.
    My best friend is a white girl named Denise—
    we look at boys together. She sat in front of me
    all through grade school because of our names:
    O'Connor, Ozawa. I know the back of Denise's head very well.
    I tell her she's going bald. She tells me I copy on tests.
    We're best friends.

    I saw Denise today in Geography class.
    She was sitting on the other side of the room.
    "You're trying to start a war," she said "giving secrets
    away to the Enemy, Why can't you keep your big
    mouth shut?"

    I didn't know what to say.
    I gave her a packet of tomato seeds
    and asked her to plant them for me, told her
    when the first tomato ripened
    she'd miss me.

134

➤ Rewrite some aspect of your own incident as a poem. Concentrate on making use of imagery and other poetic techniques that help compress your story.

135

Many poems retell incidents concisely, focusing on key details and using tone to great effect.

Four

Vignette as Commentary

Vignettes are short episodes or scenes. A **vignette** relies heavily on visual **imagery** to leave an impression—it can be compared to a photograph. It is brief because more information would complicate it without adding anything. John Sanford is a writer who uses vignettes to reconstruct moments of historical importance. *The Winters of That Country* is a series of vignettes about important events in United States history. One about the internment is called "Shikata Ga Nai," a Japanese saying meaning "What happened, happened."

"Shikata Ga Nai" from ***The Winters of That Country*** by John Sanford

← Response notes →

What happened, happened.
—Japanese saying

They wore tags, all of them, a narrow strip of cardboard hanging from a button by a string, and coming along a street somewhere, or plodding across a bridge, they might've been goods in motion, a procession of merchandise offering itself for sale. The elderly, as in a will-less dream, drifted with the flow of the young, and toylike children were buoyant on the stream. Passing before the curious at the wayside, they might've been wares on display, a showing of faces, fashions, but only the children stared back at blue-eyed staring.

The ticketed people were on their way to banishment, but not beyond the pale of their country: their place of exile lay within it, at an inner confine called Topaz, Tule, Manzanar, and they were moving now toward its towns in the desert, toward league-long reaches of mesquite and ocotillo, toward shimmering scrims of heat and winds that were made of dust. They were headed for trains of passé cars, days and nights of empty views, for a compound called Minidoka, Gila, Heart Mountain, deep inside the compound land. Their tar-paper mansions waited under the sun, black ovens, and they'd sleep in wet-down sheets and bleed from the nose in the heat. Infants would wilt and die, and blistered by blown sand, families and friends would bury them among the creosote bushes, and on a stone some day one would be known as Jerry.

It would not be long before the old ones sat gazing off into the distance as if there were nothing near they cared to see. They'd look out across scrub and sage at a dim sierra, a wedgwood band at the base of the sky. They'd sit quite still in the midst of movement, they'd be unaware of the roundabout commotion, hear none of the cries and collisions, none of the running feet, and not a word would be heard of the traffic on the air. They'd be somewhere in the far blue mountains: their past, the best of life, was there.

The young, if they dreamt at all, would dream at night: their days would hold no bygone vistas. There'd be shacks to mend, doors that didn't fit, cracks in the shrunken floors. Who would moon over blue buttes and pompous clouds when there were snakes to roust and centipedes? There'd be winds to deal with and force-fed dust, there'd be the range of the seasons, the mile-high heat and cold, there'd be

"Shikata Ga Nai" from *The Winters of That Country* by John Sanford

barrens to claim, sand-burs to burn, thistle, arrowgrass, and there'd   ← *Response notes* →
be a need to learn and wait.

The price-tagged children in doll-size clothes wouldn't know that
watch-towers weren't trees. They'd suppose they simply grew as
they'd grown, with ladders instead of branches and lamps instead of
leaves. Nor would they know that warnings were on the walls, signs
on the wire, tethers on their perfect feet. They'd play, shrill, sit in the
sand and seem to think, they'd chatter at the soldiers and never know
they were guards who'd kill. They'd never be afraid, never be sad,
bereft, abused, and yet one day (shikata ga nai) they'd begin to hate:
what happened would happen to them.

Discuss with others the impressions that stay with you after reading this vignette.
Look at Sanford's images. What effect do they have on you?

●◆ Now try drawing a snapshot of the scene Sanford has created.

137

Vignettes
are short
episodes or scenes
that rely on visual
imagery and
description. They
create a picture in the
reader's mind and
provide indirect
commentary from
the writer.

David Guterson's novel *Snow Falling on Cedars* takes place on San Piedro Island in Puget Sound in 1941 and 1950. Guterson is telling how the islanders lived in relation to one another after the internment ripped the community apart and cut off their trust of one another. In the following excerpt, he describes the inner thoughts of a Japanese American high school senior named Hatsue in 1941.

from ***Snow Falling on Cedars*** by David Guterson

← *Response notes* →

Deep among the trees she lay on a fallen log and gazed far up branchless trunks. A late winter wind blew the tops around, inducing in her a momentary vertigo. She admired a Douglas fir's complicated bark, followed its grooves to the canopy of branches two hundred feet above. The world was incomprehensibly intricate, and yet this forest made a simple sense in her heart that she felt nowhere else.

She drew up for herself, in the silence of her mind, a list of the things now cluttering her heart—her father was gone, arrested by the FBI for keeping dynamite in his shed; there was talk going around that before too long everyone with a Japanese face on San Piedro would be sent away until the war was done; she had a *hakujin* boyfriend she could see only in secret, who in a few short months was sure to be drafted and sent to kill the people of her blood. And now, on top of these insoluble things, her mother had only hours before probed into the pit of her soul and discovered her deep uncertainty. Her mother seemed to know about the gulf that separated how she lived from what she was. And what was she anyway? She was of this place and she was not of this place, and though she might desire to be an American it was clear, as her mother said, that she had the face of America's enemy and would always have such a face. She would never feel at home here among the *hakujin*, and at the same time she loved the woods and fields of home as dearly as anyone could. She had one foot in her parents' home, and from there it was not far at all to the Japan they had left behind years before. She could feel how this country far across the ocean pulled on her and lived inside her despite her wishes to the contrary; it was something she could not deny. And at the same time her feet were planted on San Piedro Island, and she wanted only her own strawberry farm, the fragrance of the fields and the cedar trees, and to live simply in this place forever. And then there was Ishmael. He was as much a part of her life as the trees, and he smelled of them and of the clam beaches. And yet he left this hole inside of her. He was not Japanese, and they had met at such a young age, their love had come out of thoughtlessness and impulse, she had fallen into loving him long before she knew herself, though it occurred to her now that she might never know herself, that perhaps no one ever does, that such a thing might not be possible. And she thought she understood what she had long sought to understand, that she concealed her love for Ishmael Chambers not

from *Snow Falling on Cedars* by David Guterson

←—Response notes—→

because she was Japanese in her heart but because she could not in truth profess to the world that what she felt for him was love at all.

She felt a sickness overtake her. Her late-afternoon walks had not concealed her meeting with a boy her mother had long had intuition of. Hatsue knew she had not fooled anybody, she had not fooled herself, as it turned out, either, she had never felt completely right. How could they say, she and Ishmael, that they truly loved each other? They had simply grown up together, been children together, and the proximity of it, the closeness of it, had produced in them love's illusion. And yet—on the other hand—what was love if it wasn't the instinct she felt to be on the moss inside the cedar tree with this boy she had always known? He was the boy of this place, of these woods, these beaches, the boy who smelled like this forest. If identity was geography instead of blood—if living in a place was what really mattered—then Ishmael was part of her, inside of her, as much as anything Japanese.

Fictional stories often rely on an **omniscient narrator** who can see and know everything. Writers also use **stream of consciousness**—writing out the flow of thoughts running through the mind of the character. Guterson's story comes from history, but he dramatizes the situation by using both of these techniques. Reread the passage, examining how each technique reveals and dramatizes Hatsue's situation.

On the chart below, write quotes that are particularly strong examples of each technique. Then, indicate what you learned from the specific examples.

Examples of Stream of Consciousness	What You Learned
"a list of the things now cluttering her heart"	Know that she has much to think about

Examples of Omniscient Narrator	What You Learned
"She admired a Douglas fir's . . ."	The world seems complicated, but she finds peace in the forest.

●◆ Use an omniscient narrator and stream of consciousness to dramatize the situation you wrote about in the first three lessons. Describe what goes on in the person's mind in trying to decide what to do. Model the techniques Guterson employs if they help you.

Writers who fictionalize historical events often use omniscient narrators and stream of consciousness to emphasize or dramatize the aspects of the real situation that they can imagine but cannot actually know.

Story Structures

Writers generally begin to work with just an idea or a situation, rather than with an entire story in mind. From this seed, a writer will construct an entire narrative by asking questions. Where does the story start and end? What is the chronology of events? What storytelling techniques suit this story? flashbacks? foreshadowing? other structuring devices? From these initial ideas about structure, a writer determines the overall design and plot of the story.

The structure affects the way you, as the reader, make sense of and react to the story. The structure affects what ideas, actions, and characters are emphasized. The structure orders the story so the reader can walk along the street one moment, enter the mind of a character the next, and then see a hawk suspended in the sky. One way of thinking about the effectiveness of a story, then, is to identify the choices writers make in structuring the story.

One As the Story Begins and Ends

Writers need to figure out effective ways to capture readers' attention. The beginning is the hook that brings the reader into the world of the story. Then at the end, the writer will provide a resolution, share an insight, or show how things have changed as a result of what happened. The beginning and ending of the story provide the frame for the story's meaning.

"A Lady's Beaded Bag" by Tennessee Williams

← Response notes →

Through the chill of a November evening a small man trudged down an alley, bearing upon his shoulders a huge, bulging sack. He moved with that uneasy, half-unconscious stealth characteristic of an old and weary mongrel who realizes that his life can be preserved from its enemies through wariness alone. The profession which he followed was not illegitimate; he had no need of fearing molestation from the enforcers of the law. And yet his manner seemed to indicate a sense of guilt and fear of detection. He kept close to the walls of the garages as though seeking concealment in their shadows. He skirted widely the circles of radiance cast by the occasional alley lights. Whenever he encountered another alleywalker he lowered his head without glancing at the other's face. He had none of the defiant hardness and boldness common among most of his kind. He was oppressed with an almost maniacal sense of lowliness and shame.

He had been a trash-picker for fifteen years. He had spent each day following an unvarying route through the alleys of the city's exclusive residential section, delving among the contents of ash-pits for old shoes, broken and rusted metal objects, and bundles of soiled and ragged cloth. The fruits of his scavangery he sold for a pittance to dealers who could make use of such rubbish. It would have been an intolerably drear and colorless occupation had he not been sustained through all of those fifteen years by the hope of some day discovering among the trash something of great worth accidentally thrown there. A diamond ring or pin, a watch, earrings—something for which he might receive hundreds of dollars, bringing the fulfillment of his beggar-dreams.

There had been times when his heart had been made to leap simply by the sharp glitter of a bit of broken glass or golden tinfoil, glimpsed over the edge of an ash-pit. And though he had found nothing as yet of greater worth than the scraps of metal, leather, and cloth, hope had not died in him.

He had made it an inviolable rule always to complete his route. Therefore, though his sack was already packed to its capacity, he would not turn back this evening until he had traversed the last block of alley. With aching feet and back he trudged from pit to pit, stopping sometimes to exchange one piece of rubbish in his bag for another of slightly more value. He came at length to a pit whose contents were surmounted by a mauve-colored milliner's box, filled with a bundle of wrapping paper. He was prompted by some impulse to pull the box to

"A Lady's Beaded Bag" by Tennessee Williams

the edge of the pit to look at it more closely. The sound of something heavy sliding beneath the bundled paper caught his attention. Removing the paper, he peered sharply into the interior of the box. He saw there one of those things for which he had been searching fifteen years. It was a lady's beaded bag.

For a moment greed was stronger than caution. With trembling fingers he seized the bag and started to lift it from its covert. But at that moment a door slammed and he quickly lifted the heel of an old shoe and pretended to examine it, while his heart hammered at his breast and his head swam with excitement. A lady's beaded bag!

The door slammed once more. He dropped the old heel, crouched closer against the pit. He reached once more into the interior of the box and found the beaded bag. He drew his fingers over its soft, cool surface with the lightness of a cautious Don Juan caressing a woman of whom he is not sure. Once more he scanned the vista of backyards before him to assure himself that he was unobserved; then with lightning speed removed the bag from the box and stuffed it into the pocket of his coat. It was done. The treasure was his.

The beginning of a story often provides the background information that will be important for the reader to know. Characters and situations are introduced and suspense created.

What did you learn in the opening paragraphs of "A Lady's Beaded Bag"? What hints are provided as to what might happen? Write down several of the impressions that you have after reading the opening paragraphs.

143

With elaborately affected nonchalance he swung the sack over his shoulder and started slowly down the alley, betraying outwardly no sign that he had found in the pit anything of more importance than the milliner's box and the old heel that he had fingered. But in his pocket his hand was clasping the beaded bag—clasping it tightly, as though only through the cutting of the tiny cool beads into the hot flesh of his palm could he be made really to believe in its reality. With his fingers he found the opening of the bag. He squeezed them into its plushy interior. He could feel the coins and bills which it contained. It was fairly stuffed with them. Enchanting visions of the pleasures which this money could bring him passed kaleidoscopically before his eyes. He pictured himself clad in handsome clothes, dining upon delectable foods, enjoying for a while those luxuries and splendors of life of which he had yearningly dreamt for many years.

Before reaching the end of the alley he glanced once more behind him. And in the instant of that glance all of his rapturous dreams were shattered. Standing beside the ash-pit in which the bag had lain was a tall young man in the garb of a chauffeur. Their eyes met. And though the regard of the young chauffeur was perfectly casual, it brought panic to the trash-picker. He fancied that he could read in that regard a cold and stern accusation. The loss of the bag, he decided, must have been discovered; it had been traced to the ash-pit. The chauffeur had been sent by his mistress to retrieve it. In all probability, he knew that it had been taken by the trash-picker. He would notify the police. And the world of which the trash-picker had always been so insanely fearful would lay its cold, cruel hands upon him for having become a violater of its laws. The thought of that made him sick with terror; frantic as a small animal caught in a trap.

Of a sudden it occured to his distracted mind that he might still save himself by surrendering the bag to its owner. Without another thought he hastened out of the alley and around the corner. He followed the walk until he came before a handsome residence of gray stone which he identified as the one in whose ash-pit he had found the bag. Almost breathless with fear and awe, he scurried up its walk and steps to the grilled outer doors. He found the bell and gave it a brief ring. In a few moments the doors were opened up on a brightly lighted vestibule and he beheld hazily a young woman clad in an austerely cut uniform of black and white.

Barely raising his eyes to her face he lifted the bag, humbly as a priest would lift an offering to the altar of some wrathful god, and mumbled,

"I found this in the trash."

Looking at the bag, the maid recognized it as one belonging to her employer. She realized that it must have been thrown in the trash-pit with the milliner's box which she had removed from her employer's room that morning. She feared, however, that she might be dismissed for carelessness should she tell the true circumstances of its loss and recovery. Therefore, upon bringing the bag to her employer's bed-room, where she was dressing for a dinner engagement, she said,

"A Lady's Beaded Bag" by Tennessee Williams

←Response notes→

"Mrs. Ferrabye, I found this lying on the piano."

Without turning from her dressing table at which she was arranging her hair, the woman replied,

"Put it in my drawer, Hilda."

A few minutes later a delivery man arrived with a belated package from a modiste's shop. The maid carried it up to her employer's room, laid it on the bed and gave her employer the bill. It amounted to several hundred dollars. The woman opened her beaded bag. She drew out that sum—practically all that the bag contained—and handed it to the maid. Then she lifted the lid of the box and raised from its tissue wrappings an evening wrap of diaphanous white material, sprinkled with glistening bits of metal. She held it beneath the light to survey it critically a moment; then dropped it upon the bed, marring the refined beauty of her face with a grimace of disgust.

"Honestly, I must have been out of my mind when I bought this thing. Why I could never dream of wearing anything so perfectly ridiculous."

Turning back to the mirror and beginning once more to smooth the golden coils of her hair, her momentary annoyance passed, and her face quickly resumed its former expression of smiling self-satisfaction.

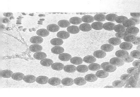

●◆Examine how the beginning and ending work together in this story. In the left column of the chart below, list quotes, key actions, or images that are introduced in the beginning and have significance later. In the middle column, explain how they are reintroduced at the end. In the right column, explain the significance of each to the meaning of the story.

In the Beginning	At the End	Significance
the small man's wariness	"almost breathless with fear"	afraid to take chances

The beginning of a story prepares the reader for whatever experiences and actions follow. The ending shows the significance of even the smallest detail, image, or action.

Two
Suspense Through Foreshadowing

Suspense keeps the reader unsettled, anticipating what will happen as the story unfolds. **Foreshadowing** causes the reader to alternate between recognizing a hint, making judgments about what it means, and finding further hints that provide resolution or more suspense. Foreshadowing is created by descriptions, questions, images, objects, and **repetitions** that hint at what is still to come or what is significant. Reread a "A Lady's Beaded Bag," marking where you find foreshadowing.

Choose four examples of foreshadowing. Describe each in detail, in the order of their occurrence, in the boxes below. What does the subject of the foreshadowing have to do with the outcome of the story? How does this particular foreshadowing episode affect your reaction to the story?

1.

Subject/Outcome:

Reaction:

2.

Subject/Outcome:

Reaction:

3.

Subject/Outcome:

Reaction:

4.

Subject/Outcome:

Reaction:

146

Foreshadowing is a structural device used to create suspense and maintain the reader's involvement in the story.

Compare your chart with that of a partner. Discuss how you think each example contributes to the tension in the story.

Three
Flashbacks

In a movie, it is easy to know when a **flashback** occurs. The image on the screen dissolves and we drop back in time for a sequence of action that explains a character's previous life or gives background on the present situation. Flashbacks in literature require more careful structuring. Sense perceptions often trigger flashbacks—the smell of oysters, the taste of a cookie, the sight of a fire truck or a yellow rose—that recall for the character something out of the past. Positioning the flashback sequences requires careful thought. In Ralph Ellison's short story "Flying Home," the narrator, Todd, has crashed his plane and suffered serious injuries. He drifts in and out of consciousness while waiting for fellow pilots to rescue him.

from **"Flying Home"** by Ralph Ellison

←—Response notes—→

Todd tensed. Was he being laughed at again? But before he could decide, the pain shook him and a part of him was lying calmly behind the screen of pain that had fallen between them, recalling the first time he had ever seen a plane. It was as though an endless series of hangars had been shaken ajar in the airbase of his memory and from each, like a young wasp emerging from its cell, arose the memory of a plane.

The first time I ever saw a plane I was very small and planes were new in the world. I was four and a half and the only plane that I had ever seen was a model suspended from the ceiling of the automobile exhibit at the state fair. But I did not know that it was only a model. I did not know how large a real plane was, nor how expensive. To me it was a fascinating toy, complete in itself, which my mother said could only be owned by rich little white boys. I stood rigid with admiration, my head straining backward as I watched the gray little plane describing arcs above the gleaming tops of the automobiles. And I vowed that, rich or poor, some day I would own such a toy. My mother had to drag me out of the exhibit, and not even the merry-go-round, the Ferris wheel, or the racing horses could hold my attention for the rest of the fair. I was too busy imitating the tiny drone of the plane with my lips, and imitating with my hands the motion, swift and circling, that it made in flight.

After that I no longer used the pieces of lumber that lay about our backyard to construct wagons and autos . . . now it was used for airplanes. I built biplanes, using pieces of board for wings, a small box for the fuselage, another piece of wood for the rudder. The trip to the fair had brought something new into my small world. I asked my mother repeatedly when the fair would come back again. I'd lie in the grass and watch the sky and each flighting bird became a soaring plane. I would have been good a year just to have seen a plane again. I became a nuisance to everyone with my questions about airplanes. But planes were new to the old folks, too, and there was little that they could tell me. Only my uncle knew some of the answers. And better still, he could carve propellers from pieces of wood that would whirl rapidly in the wind, wobbling noisily upon oiled nails.

147

I wanted a plane more than I'd wanted anything; more than I wanted the red wagon with rubber tires, more than the train that ran on a track with its train of cars. I asked my mother over and over again:

"Mama?"

"What do you want, boy?" she'd say.

"Mama, will you get mad if I ask you?" I'd say.

"What do you want now, I ain't got time to be answering a lot of fool questions. What you want?"

"Mama, when you gonna get me one . . . ?" I'd ask.

"Get you one what?" she'd say.

"You know, Mama; what I been asking you . . ."

"Boy," she'd say, "if you don't want a spanking you better come on 'n tell me what you talking about so I can get on with my work."

"Aw, Mama, you know . . ."

"What I just tell you?" she'd say.

"I mean when you gonna buy me a airplane."

"AIRPLANE! Boy, is you crazy? How many times I have to tell you to stop that foolishness. I done told you them things cost too much. I bet I'm gon wham the living daylight out of you if you don't quit worrying me 'bout them things!"

But this did not stop me, and a few days later I'd try all over again.

Then one day a strange thing happened. It was spring and for some reason I had been hot and irritable all morning. It was a beautiful spring. I could feel it as I played barefoot in the backyard. Blossoms hung from the thorny black locust trees like clusters of fragrant white grapes. Butterflies flickered in the sunlight above the short new dew-wet grass. I had gone in the house for bread and butter and coming out I heard a steady unfamiliar drone. It was unlike anything I had ever heard before. I tried to place the sound. It was no use. It was a sensation like that I had when searching for my father's watch, heard ticking unseen in a room. It made me feel as though I had forgotten to perform some task that my mother had ordered . . . then I located it, overhead. In the sky, flying quite low and about a hundred yards off, was a plane! It came so slowly that it seemed barely to move. My mouth hung wide; my bread and butter fell into the dirt. I wanted to jump up and down and cheer. And when the idea struck I trembled with excitement: Some little white boy's plane's done flew away and all I got to do is stretch out my hands and it'll be mine! It was a little plane like that at the fair, flying no higher than the eaves of our roof. Seeing it come steadily forward I felt the world grow warm with promise. I opened the screen and climbed over it and clung there, waiting. I would catch the plane as it came over and swing down fast and run into the house before anyone could see me. Then no one could come to claim the plane. It droned nearer. Then when it hung like a silver cross in the blue directly above me I stretched out my hand and grabbed. It was like sticking my finger through a soap bubble. The plane flew on, as though I had simply

148

from **"Flying Home"** by Ralph Ellison

blown my breath after it. I grabbed again, frantically, trying to catch the tail. My fingers clutched the air and disappointment surged tight and hard in my throat. Giving one last desperate grasp, I strained forward. My fingers ripped from the screen. I was falling. The ground burst hard against me. I drummed the earth with my heels and when my breath returned, I lay there bawling.

← Response notes →

Generally a flashback is structured in one of two ways—within the mind of the character or through the author's use of an **omniscient narrator**. Sometimes authors use a number of short flashbacks or, as in Ellison's story, a long, sustained flashback.

●◆ Identify several passages in the flashback that informed you about Todd's current situation. Copy them in column one of the chart below. In the right column, explain how these passages help you understand more about this character.

Key passages that reveal Todd's situation	Analysis of how the passages provide information
Learn that planes associated with white boys	Todd was early on fascinated with planes as toys and that he saw them as out of his reach.

With a partner, discuss what you learned about Todd as a character through the flashback. How effective was the flashback in revealing character?

Flashbacks break up the plot sequence of a story by moving into the past to provide relevant information or explanation.

Four
The Fork in the Road

Plot unfolds out of the decisions a character makes. Often, the character faces a "fork in the road," forcing him or her to choose one course over another. A writer includes some of the significant events that hint at the character's choices—dramatizing them to give life and complexity to the characters.

"The Far and the Near" by Thomas Wolfe

← *Response notes* →

On the outskirts of a little town upon a rise of land that swept back from the railway there was a tidy little cottage of white boards, trimmed vividly with green blinds. To one side of the house there was a garden neatly patterned with plots of growing vegetables, and an arbor for the grapes which ripened late in August. Before the house there were three mighty oaks which sheltered it in their clean and massive shade in summer, and to the other side there was a border of gay flowers. The whole place had an air of tidiness, thrift, and modest comfort.

Every day, a few minutes after two o'clock in the afternoon, the limited express between two cities passed this spot. At that moment the great train, having halted for a breathing-space at the town near by, was beginning to lengthen evenly into its stroke, but it had not yet reached the full drive of its terrific speed. It swung into view deliberately, swept past with a powerful swaying motion of the engine, a low smooth rumble of its heavy cars upon pressed steel, and then it vanished in the cut. For a moment the progress of the engine could be marked by heavy bellowing puffs of smoke that burst at spaced intervals above the edges of the meadow grass, and finally nothing could be heard but the solid clacking tempo of the wheels receding into the drowsy stillness of the afternoon.

Every day for more than twenty years, as the train had approached this house, the engineer had blown on the whistle, and every day, as soon as she heard this signal, a woman had appeared on the back porch of the little house and waved to him. At first she had a small child clinging to her skirts, and now this child had grown to full womanhood, and every day she, too, came with her mother to the porch and waved.

The engineer had grown old and gray in service. He had driven his great train, loaded with its weight of lives, across the land ten thousand times. His own children had grown up and married, and four times he had seen before him on the tracks the ghastly dot of tragedy converging like a cannon ball to its eclipse of horror at the boiler head—a light spring wagon filled with children, with its clustered row of small stunned faces; a cheap automobile stalled upon the tracks, set with the wooden figures of people paralyzed with fear; a battered hobo walking by the rail, too deaf and old to hear the whistle's warning; and a form flung past his window with a scream—all this the man had seen and known. He had known all the grief, the joy, the peril and the labor such a man could know; he had grown seamed and weathered in his loyal service, and now, schooled by the qualities of faith and courage and humbleness that attended his labor, he had grown old, and had the grandeur and the wisdom these men have.

150

"The Far and the Near" by Thomas Wolfe

But no matter what peril or tragedy he had known, the vision of the little house and the women waving to him with a brave free motion of the arm had become fixed in the mind of the engineer as something beautiful and enduring, something beyond all change and ruin, and something that would always be the same, no matter what mishap, grief or error might break the iron schedule of his days.

The sight of the little house and of these two women gave him the most extraordinary happiness he had ever known. He had seen them in a thousand lights, a hundred weathers. He had seen them through the harsh bare light of wintry gray across the brown and frosted stubble of the earth, and he had seen them again in the green luring sorcery of April.

He felt for them and for the little house in which they lived such tenderness as a man might feel for his own children, and at length the picture of their lives was carved so sharply in his heart that he felt he knew their lives completely, to every hour and moment of the day, and he resolved that one day, when his years of service should be ended, he would go and find these people and speak at last with them whose lives had been so wrought into his own.

That day came. At last the engineer stepped from a train onto the station platform of the town where these two women lived. His years upon the rail had ended. He was a pensioned servant of his company, with no more work to do. The engineer walked slowly through the station and out into the streets of the town. Everything was as strange to him as if he had never seen this town before. As he walked on, his sense of bewilderment and confusion grew. Could this be the town he had passed ten thousand times? Were these the same houses he had seen so often from the high windows of his cab? It was all as unfamiliar, as disquieting as a city in a dream, and the perplexity of his spirit increased as he went on.

Presently the houses thinned into the straggling outposts of the town, and the street faded into a country road—the one on which the women lived. And the man plodded on slowly in the heat and dust. At length he stood before the house he sought. He knew at once that he had found the proper place. He saw the lordly oaks before the house, the flower beds, the garden and the arbor, and farther off, the glint of rails.

Yes, this was the house he sought, the place he had passed so many times, the destination he had longed for with such happiness. But now that he had found it, now that he was here, why did his hand falter on the gate; why had the town, the road, the earth, the very entrance to this place he loved turned unfamiliar as the landscape of some ugly dream? Why did he now feel this sense of confusion, doubt and hopelessness?

At length he entered by the gate, walked slowly up the path and in a moment more had mounted three short steps that led up to the porch, and was knocking at the door. Presently he heard steps in the hall, the door was opened, and a woman stood facing him.

And instantly, with a sense of bitter loss and grief, he was sorry he had come. He knew at once that the woman who stood there looking at him with a mistrustful eye was the same woman who had

waved to him so many thousand times. But her face was harsh and pinched and meager; the flesh sagged wearily in sallow folds, and the small eyes peered at him with timid suspicion and uneasy doubt. All the brave freedom, the warmth and the affection that he had read into her gesture, vanished in the moment that he saw her and heard her unfriendly tongue.

And now his own voice sounded unreal and ghastly to him as he tried to explain his presence, to tell her who he was and the reason he had come. But he faltered on, fighting stubbornly against the horror of regret, confusion, disbelief that surged up in his spirit, drowning all his former joy and making his act of hope and tenderness seem shameful to him.

At length the woman invited him almost unwillingly into the house, and called her daughter in a harsh shrill voice. Then, for a brief agony of time, the man sat in an ugly little parlor, and he tried to talk while the two women stared at him with a dull, bewildered hostility, a sullen, timorous restraint.

And finally, stammering a crude farewell, he departed. He walked away down the path and then along the road toward town, and suddenly he knew that he was an old man. His heart, which had been brave and confident when it looked along the familiar vista of the rails, was now sick with doubt and horror as it saw the strange and unsuspected visage of an earth which had always been within a stone's throw of him, and which he had never seen or known. And he knew that all the magic of that bright lost way, the vista of that shining line, the imagined corner of that small good universe of hope's desire, was gone forever, could never be got back again.

152

One incident can alter a character's life. A good way to analyze how a writer structures a story to reveal "a fork in the road" is to focus on the current situation first. Then, trace back the hints the writer gives to explain how the character ended up that way. Describe the present situation, the incident, and the way things were before. Use two sentences for each description.

Present situation:

....

....

Incident:

....

....

Past situation:

....

....

➼ Since "The Far and the Near" is told from a **third-person point of** view that emphasizes the engineer's perspective, we never actually know his thoughts. Write an inner dialogue where the engineer explains what caused him to take the fork he did and why he is "now sick with doubt and horror."

153

Writers structure a story so that readers can understand what shapes a character. Most stories include a crucial point at which, or after which, a character's choices become significantly diminished.

Five Unity in the Story

The Russian writer Anton Chekhov wrote, "A shotgun introduced on page one must go off before the end of the story." Unity of effect is the organization of all a story's elements so that they enhance the total effect. A story's structure organizes the relationships between the various elements or aspects of the story. Each part functions in its relationship to the whole. What created unity in "The Far and the Near" by Thomas Wolfe?

●◆ Write your ideas about how Wolfe's title emphasizes one way that Wolfe has structured continuity into the story.

....

....

....

....

Far

Another way to understand the unity of a story is to try to envision the key scenes. Visualize what you see as the key details of the "far" and the "near" at central moments in the story. Sketch a scene for each in the boxes provided. Don't worry about artistic ability. You are using sketching as a tool for understanding unity in the title and scenes.

Near

As readers begin to sense the pattern or design of the story, they can begin to see the relationships between various elements of the plot and character.

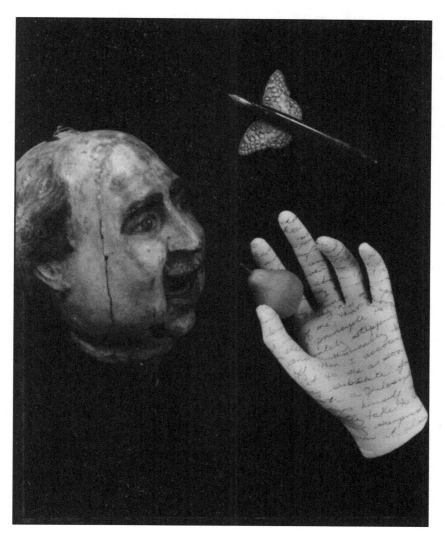

Talking Back in Poetry

Have you listened to any "talk radio" programs? You probably know that they are popular because listeners get to talk back to the host and each other. "Talking back" is deeply ingrained in the American way of thinking. For more than two hundred years, the First Amendment of the United States Constitution has guaranteed that, within certain guidelines, people can express their points of view.

Poets and other writers also love to "talk back" to each other. Writers are also readers, and they know what others have written. Wonderful literature has been written in response to other poems. Two ways of replying are through allusion and parody.

Reading to consider a poet's references to other poems can help you reach a new level of comprehension. You must immerse yourself in the poet's world and way of thinking. By doing so, you will develop an understanding of a poet's time and culture and of how they have become a part of his or her work.

Poems with short, simple words might seem easy to understand. And they are—at the literal level. The poem becomes more complex and more interesting when you look beyond the exact meanings of the words. Poems are written in a particular time and place, and that context often makes a difference to the meaning of the poem. Read "I, Too, Sing America" and concentrate on the **literal** meaning.

Response notes

I, Too, Sing America
Langston Hughes

I, too, sing America.

I am the darker brother.
They send me to eat in the kitchen
When company comes,
But I laugh,
And eat well,
And grow strong.

Tomorrow,
I'll be at the table
When company comes.
Nobody'll dare
Say to me,
"Eat in the kitchen,"
Then.

Besides,
They'll see how beautiful I am
And be ashamed—

I, too, am America.

What is your initial response to this poem? Take a few minutes to write down questions, impressions, and ideas in the response notes.

☛ Now describe what you think the poem literally means.

Langston Hughes was probably the best-known of the many artists, writers, and musicians of the Harlem Renaissance. In the 1920s, a group of writers and artists protested oppression and made other Americans aware of African American culture and life. Segregation laws were still an appalling fact of life; Hughes wrote, "Most of my own poems are racial in theme and treatment and derived from the life I know."

Reread "I, Too, Sing America." Speculate on the relationship between the speaker and his culture. Fill in the inference chart with details from the poem and the inferences you make from the details.

Details about the speaker and culture	Inferences
"darker brother"	probably an African American

157

●◆ Explain what you think Hughes meant by "They'll see how beautiful I am / And be ashamed"?

Knowing the era and culture of a poem provides an additional perspective for understanding the meaning.

Two Understanding Allusions

Langston Hughes's "I, Too, Sing America" was a reply to a poem published by Walt Whitman in 1860. Talking back to an earlier poem in this way is a form of **allusion.** An allusion is a concise way of suggesting additional meaning to the reader who knows both works. Writers may refer directly or indirectly to a figure, event, character, author, work, and so on. In this case, when you read the two poems together you should end up with a fuller understanding of each of them.

The poetry of Walt Whitman probably does not seem unusual today. However, he truly shocked readers in the nineteenth century. Both the form and content of his poems disturbed people who had fixed ideas about what a poem should be. Whitman believed that a poet in a democracy should speak for all of the people. He also believed that he should use a **verse form** that did not restrict him.

Listen to someone read "I Hear America Singing."

Response notes

I Hear America Singing
Walt Whitman

I hear America singing, the varied carols I hear,
Those of mechanics, each one singing his as it
    should be blithe and strong,
The carpenter singing his as he measures his
    plank or beam,
The mason singing his as he makes ready for
    work, or leaves off work,
The boatman singing what belongs to him in his
    boat, the deckhand singing on the steamboat deck,
The shoemaker singing as he sits on his bench,
    the hatter singing as he stands,
The wood-cutter's song, the ploughboy's on his way
    in the morning, or at noon intermission or at sundown,
The delicious singing of the mother, or of the young
    wife at work, or of the girl sewing or washing,
Each singing what belongs to him or her and to
    none else,
The day what belongs to the day—at night the
    party of young fellows, robust, friendly,
Singing with open mouths their strong melodious
    songs.

Now read the poem to yourself and note each person or type of person who is singing. All except the young men in the last lines seem to be celebrating one thing. Write down what that is in the response notes. Discuss your answer in a group to learn what Whitman's theme and perspective are.

●◆ **What is Whitman literally saying in this poem?**

Now, analyze the poems by Whitman and Hughes. Complete the following chart.

	Whitman	Hughes
form of the poem		few words, short lines, sharp contrasts between "I" and "they," repetition
title		
use of "sing" and "singing"		
topic		
tone	optimistic, joyous	
poet's stance	observer	

●◆ **What is Hughes saying to Whitman and the world of readers by his allusion?**

> Knowing that a poet is alluding to a previous work provides an additional perspective for understanding both poems.

The title of Langston Hughes's poem lets the reader know that he is replying to Whitman. Poets often include **allusions** within the lines of their poems rather than in the title. Sometimes they allude to more than one previous event, literary work, or person.

The writers' reasons for making allusions vary. Hughes's poem makes readers aware that Whitman's vision of America could be expanded. Sara Henderson Hay's sonnet, "One of the Seven Has Somewhat to Say," draws on a well-known fairy tale as its source.

Response notes

One of the Seven Has Somewhat to Say
Sara Henderson Hay

Remember how it was before she came—?
The picks and shovels dropped beside the door,
The sink piled high, the meals any old time,
Our jackets where we'd flung them on the floor?
The mud tracked in, the clutter on the shelves,
None of us shaved, or more than halfway clean . . .
Just seven old bachelors, living by ourselves?
Those were the days, if you know what I mean.

She scrubs, she sweeps, she even dusts the ceilings;
She's made us build a tool shed for our stuff.
Dinner's at eight, the table setting's formal.
And if I weren't afraid I'd hurt her feelings
I'd move, until we get her married off,
And things can gradually slip back to normal.

●►Discuss this poem with a partner. Who is "she"? Who is the speaker? How does the speaker feel? Write your answers below.

....

....

....

....

....

....

....

Did you recognize this as the story of Snow White and the Seven Dwarfs? In that story, a jealous stepmother sends a servant into the woods to kill young, beautiful Snow White. He cannot do it and leaves her there. She wanders until evening when she comes upon a little cottage. Everything inside is clean and tidy. She eats a little of the food that is set out on the table and lies down on one of the seven beds. In come the dwarfs who assure her that, if she will cook and clean for them, they will protect her from the evil queen. But one day the evil stepmother tricks her into eating a poisoned apple. Thinking that she is dead, the dwarfs build her a glass coffin, and, eventually, a prince comes to wake her and take her away. They presumably, in the best fairy tale fashion, live happily ever after.

●◆ On one level, Hay's poem is an amusing look at a traditional story. But she is also making a more subtle point. Choose one of the two sentences below and write a paragraph supporting it.

1. By alluding to the story of Snow White, Hay makes a contemporary statement about differences between the attitudes of men and women.

2. Hay is more sympathetic to the woman in the poem than to the speaker.

161

A poet can use an allusion to make a statement about contemporary attitudes.

Four

Talking Back with Parody

Parody is a humorous way of talking back. Editorial cartoons and caricatures are visual forms of **parody**. You also may have seen parodies on television shows such as *Saturday Night Live*. Literary parodies may be prose or poetry, but they are usually written in the same genre as the original work. Poetic parodies are often humorous or lightly mocking as the writers exaggerate or distort the features of the text they are parodying. To write a good parody, writers need to understand and appreciate the original.

Response notes

This Is Just to Say
William Carlos Williams

I have eaten
the plums
that were in
the icebox

and which
you were probably
saving
for breakfast

Forgive me
they were delicious
so sweet
and so cold

Williams believed that poetry should be written in the language of everyday speech. He also felt that it should concentrate on concrete details rather than abstract ideas. "This Is Just to Say" is about a common situation. One way to understand the situation better is to imagine that you are the "you" of the poem. Write a note back to the speaker of the poem. Tell him or her just how you feel about the action of eating the plums.

Now, read a parody of "This Is Just to Say."

Variations on a Theme by William Carlos Williams
Kenneth Koch

Response notes

1
I chopped down the house that you had been saving to live in
  next summer.
I am sorry, but it was morning, and I had nothing to do
and its wooden beams were so inviting.

2
We laughed at the hollyhocks together
And then I sprayed them with lye.
Forgive me. I simply do not know what I am doing.

3
I gave away the money that you had been saving to live on
  for the next ten years.
The man who asked for it was shabby
and the firm March wind on the porch was so juicy and cold.

4
Last evening we went dancing and I broke your leg.
Forgive me. I was clumsy, and
I wanted you here in the wards, where I am the doctor!

●◆ What evidence is there that Koch understands and appreciates "This Is Just to Say"? Use a Venn diagram to compare the poems. Put any similarities in the space where the circles overlap. Put differences in the rest of the circles.

Williams

Koch

A good writer of parodies must understand and appreciate the original. An active reader needs to understand how the two works compare and contrast to understand the parody.

163

Five
Analyzing a Parody

Reread the poems by William Carlos Williams and Kenneth Koch. You may have noticed that "Variations on a Theme by William Carlos Williams" varies not only the **theme** but also the structure. Analyzing these variations will help you see how Koch makes us see the Williams poem differently.

Williams's poem has three **stanzas** with a distinct focus in each one. Complete the chart below to analyze Koch's variations. Once the chart is completed, you will be able to see what he has exaggerated or distorted from the original. By the way, Williams was a doctor in addition to being a poet. Knowing that may help you understand the last line of Koch's poem.

Sections of Williams's poem	Koch's details, by stanza	What is exaggerated
confession	1. 2. 3. 4.	
importance of the object to the other person	1. "house that you had been saving to live in" 2. killed hollyhocks that the two people had enjoyed 3. "money that you had been saving to live on" 4. "I broke your leg"	The importance of each of these objects is much more serious than the plums were in Williams's poem. The house and the money represent security, and the hollyhocks and broken leg could represent that there's something wrong with their relationship.
request for forgiveness and excuse	1. 2. 3. 4.	

Writing a parody is another way that poets talk back to each other. Parodies follow the style of the original but also comment on it.

Modern Interpretations of Myth

The first meaning of *interpret* in *The American Heritage Dictionary* is "to explain to oneself the meaning of; elucidate." Interpretation is not some school-based thing that you do; it is just what we all do whenever we are faced with something that is not crystal clear. We explain it to ourselves. We make sense of it. Then we can talk about it to others. Talking about it may alter our own understanding or change our interpretation. Interpretation is an ongoing process; it is never finished.

Myths provide us with endless opportunities to write about things that are important to us. Writers return again and again to myths as a basis for making comments on our lives. Shifting perspective, writers can probe meanings behind stories that we know from only one point of view. In myths, writers have stories that can be told over and over again, stories open to endless interpretation.

Titles, which are often skipped over, give you essential information. If you do not read the title or know what it means, you may still be able to make some meaning from the lines, but not as much. Read the following poem without its title and see what you can make of it.

Response notes

In the pathway of the sun,
  In the footsteps of the breeze,
Where the world and sky are one,
  He shall ride the silver seas,
    He shall cut the glittering wave.
I shall sit at home, and rock;
Rise, to heed a neighbor's knock;
Brew my tea, and snip my thread;
Bleach the linen for my bed.
    They will call him brave.

What can you say about the speaker of this poem?

....

....

....

....

....

The poem was written by Dorothy Parker in the 1930s and is called "Penelope." How does knowing this add to or change your ideas about the speaker of the poem?

....

....

....

....

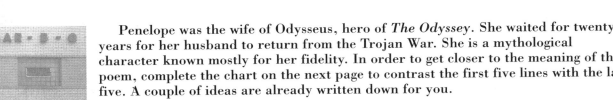

Penelope was the wife of Odysseus, hero of *The Odyssey*. She waited for twenty years for her husband to return from the Trojan War. She is a mythological character known mostly for her fidelity. In order to get closer to the meaning of the poem, complete the chart on the next page to contrast the first five lines with the last five. A couple of ideas are already written down for you.

	Language (look especially at the connotations of the words)	Tone (contrast positive and negative aspects)	Roles in Society (contrast roles of men and women as portrayed in poem)
Lines 1–5	"ride the silver seas" sounds exotic and daring	exciting	the man is off doing exciting things
Lines 6–10			

167

Collect your ideas about the following questions.

•◆ Why do you think Parker titled this poem "Penelope"?

•◆ Who are "they" in the last line of the poem? What is Penelope's attitude in this line?

•◆ Would it have been as strong a poem, making the same points, without the title? Explain your answer.

> The title of a poem is essential for placing the reader in the world of the poem. It is often the reader's best clue to what the poet is commenting on.

•◆ What do you think is the meaning of the poem?

Two Making Connections

E. M. Forster was quoted as saying "Only connect." What he meant was that we should focus on what a writer is trying to say about our lives. The urge to connect is strong. When we read, we automatically connect what we are reading with our own experience. It is when we cannot make those connections that the literature seems dry and uninteresting. Read Edna St. Vincent Millay's poem "An Ancient Gesture," noting any connections you can make to this poem.

Response notes

An Ancient Gesture
Edna St. Vincent Millay

I thought, as I wiped my eyes on the corner of my apron:
Penelope did this too.
And more than once: you can't keep weaving all day
And undoing it all through the night;
Your arms get tired, and the back of your neck gets tight;
And along towards morning, when you think it will never
   be light,
And your husband has been gone, and you don't know
   where, for years,
Suddenly you burst into tears;
There is simply nothing else to do.

And I thought, as I wiped my eyes on the corner of my
   apron:
This is an ancient gesture, authentic, antique,
In the very best tradition, classic, Greek;
Ulysses did this too.
But only as a gesture,—a gesture which implied
To the assembled throng that he was much too moved to
   speak.
He learned it from Penelope . . .
Penelope, who really cried.

168

During the time Penelope waited for Odysseus, she was pursued by many suitors who thought Odysseus dead and wanted his land and power. Unable to keep putting them off, Penelope promised that she would decide among them when she finished weaving a shroud for her father-in-law. So she wove during the day, and at night, while the suitors slept, she unraveled all that she had woven during the day. This ruse kept them at bay until Odysseus finally returned.

What connections does Millay make with Penelope?

What do you think Millay wants us to understand by the word *really* in the last line?

Compare Millay's poem with Dorothy Parker's from the previous lesson. In what ways are they making similar statements? How do they differ? Which one do you think is more effective? Why?

169

It is important to recognize when a writer is employing an older story or a myth in a poem. Knowing the original allows you to see how the writer is reinterpreting and commenting on older stories.

Three

Ancient Myths in Modern Dress

Poets like to play with established stories and put them in contemporary **settings** and language. In this way, they bring out the meaning that **myths** still have for us. The sirens were mythical monsters, half woman and half bird. Greek poets wrote that they sang so sweetly that seamen attempting to sail by the rock on which they lived forgot everything and died of hunger. Read Margaret Atwood's "Siren Song" and see what the sirens have to say to us today.

Response notes

Siren Song
Margaret Atwood

This is the one song everyone
would like to learn: the song
that is irresistible:

the song that forces men
to leap overboard in squadrons
even though they see the beached skulls

the song nobody knows
because anyone who has heard it
is dead, and the others can't remember.

Shall I tell you the secret
and if I do, will you get me
out of this bird suit?

I don't enjoy it here
squatting on this island
looking picturesque and mythical

with these two feathery maniacs,
I don't enjoy singing
this trio, fatal and valuable.

I will tell the secret to you,
to you, only to you.
Come closer. This song

is a cry for help: Help me!
Only you, only you can,
you are unique

at last. Alas
it is a boring song
but it works every time.

Discuss the following questions with a partner or small group:

●◆ Who is the speaker?

●◆ Who is the "you" in the poem?

●◆ What happens to the "you"?

●◆ What "works every time"?

●◆ Notice Atwood's use of language. Cite some examples of contemporary usage in the poem.

●◆ What is the effect of this kind of language in a poem dealing with a myth?

◗ Now, write your ideas about the point that Atwood is making. What does the poem say about men and women in our society? What does it say about gullibility? about manipulation? What is the effect of using characters from myth to make these points? Be as explicit as you can in saying what you think about both the meaning and the language of this poem.

Contemporary language makes it easy for us to see the meaning of a myth in our own times.

Four
Changing the Tone of a Myth

The story of Demeter and her daughter was an ancient Greek explanation of the seasons. Hades, the god of the underworld, fell in love with Persephone, the daughter of Demeter, goddess of the harvest. He kidnapped Persephone and made her queen of the underworld. Demeter mourned her loss, and the earth fell into winter and no food could be grown. Alarmed by this, Zeus, the king of the gods, arranged for Persephone to spend part of each year with her mother and part with Hades. The earth blossoms when Persephone is with her mother, but during winter when Persephone is in the underworld and Demeter mourns, no plants grow.

Demeter's Prayer to Hades
Rita Dove

This alone is what I wish for you: knowledge.
To understand each desire and its edge,
to know we are responsible for the lives
we change. No faith comes without cost,
no one believes without dying.
Now for the first time
I see clearly the trail you planted,
what ground opened to waste,
though you dreamed a wealth
of flowers.

       There are no curses, only mirrors
held up to the souls of gods and mortals.
And so I give up this fate, too.
Believe in yourself,
go ahead—see where it gets you.

Response notes

173

●◖ Although Demeter is speaking to Hades, it seems clear from the **tone** that the speaker of the poem is using the myth to speak to a broader, contemporary audience. What do you think about the line "we are responsible for the lives we change"? Give an example from today's society that might support or refute the meaning of that line.

●◆ Although this poem builds on the story of a myth, its language indicates a very modern message. What is Demeter saying here? Rewrite her prayer to Hades line by line. Where it seems to work, you may keep some of her words in your version.

DEMETER'S PRAYER TO HADES   *Your Version*

This alone is what I wish for you: knowledge.

To understand each desire and its edge,

to know we are responsible for the lives

we change. No faith comes without cost,

no one believes without dying.

Now for the first time

I see clearly the trail you planted,

what ground opened to waste,

though you dreamed a wealth

of flowers.

      There are no curses, only mirrors

held up to the souls of gods and mortals.

And so I give up this fate, too.

Believe in yourself,

go ahead—see where it gets you.

Do not be misled by the apparent subject of a poem. Look for the tone of the poem to give you insight into the possibilities of meaning in poetry.

Five
Changing Perspective

Writers often retell myths in order to examine the story from a different **point of view**. In the following poem, Muriel Rukeyser imagines a dialogue between Oedipus as an old man and the Sphinx. When Oedipus was a young man, he had solved the riddle of the Sphinx. His triumph gave way to tragedy, however, as Oedipus gradually learned that, unknowingly, he had killed his father and married his mother. Here is Rukeyser's view of the retrospective dialogue.

Myth
Muriel Rukeyser

Response notes

Long afterward, Oedipus, old and blinded, walked the
roads.   He smelled a familiar smell.   It was
the Sphinx.   Oedipus said, "I want to ask one question.
Why didn't I recognize my mother?"   "You gave the
wrong answer," said the Sphinx.   "But that was what
made everything possible," said Oedipus.   "No," she said.
"When I asked, What walks on four legs in the morning,
two at noon, and three in the evening, you answered,
Man.   You didn't say anything about woman."
"When you say Man," said Oedipus, "you include women
too. Everyone knows that."   She said, "That's what
you think."

175

●◆ The ending of the poem makes this a very contemporary feminist statement.
Describe the point of view of the poem.

●◆Go back now to Rita Dove's poem "Demeter's Prayer to Hades" in Lesson Four. Imagine that you are writing from the perspective of Hades. You have seen a beautiful young woman and carried her off to the underworld to be your bride. Write a short poetic monologue from the point of view of Hades speaking to Persephone's angry mother Demeter.

Changing point of view or perspective can give you new insights into well-known stories.

Writing from Models

Poets get ideas from their experiences, their observations, their reading. One way many poets get started writing, either as beginners or professionals, is to model their writing on other poems. Modeling takes many forms, from the closely modeled word-for-word emulation to very loose models that may use a line or two from the original. Sometimes poets use another poem as a springboard. Sometimes they write an answer to it. Sometimes they borrow the first line and go on from there. The possibilities are endless.

Writing poems in what are called fixed forms—the sonnet, for example—is almost like modeling. You write to a preconceived pattern that sets up the number of lines, line length or meter, and rhyme scheme.

The world of poetry is filled with poets writing poems to each other, about each other, about poetry, about the difficulties of writing, about the ecstasies of writing. If you think of modeling as professional writers do—as playing with language, following forms, and creating forms—you will have a good time trying your hand at these exercises.

Edwin Arlington Robinson based his poem "Richard Cory" on a very human weakness, envy. The poem is appealing because most of us have experienced this emotion at one time or another. As you read the poem, write your comments and questions in the response notes.

Response notes

Richard Cory
Edwin Arlington Robinson

Whenever Richard Cory went down town,
We people on the pavement looked at him:
He was a gentleman from sole to crown,
Clean favored and imperially slim.

And he was always quietly arrayed,
And he was always human when he talked;
But still he fluttered pulses when he said,
"Good-morning," and he glittered when he walked.

And he was rich—yes, richer than a king—
And admirably schooled in every grace:
In fine, we thought that he was everything
To make us wish that we were in his place.

So on we worked, and waited for the light,
And went without the meat and cursed the bread;
And Richard Cory, one calm summer night,
Went home and put a bullet through his head.

178

Discuss these questions with a partner or group:
• Who is the narrator of the poem?
• What do you know about him?
• What do you know about Richard Cory?
• What do you not know about him?

You are going to write a poem modeled on "Richard Cory" using your own character. Think of a person who seems to have everything that most teenagers would want. Make up a name for your character (do not use a real person). Plan a final, surprising twist for your poem.

➥ Begin your poem as shown below.

Whenever (insert your character's name) went (insert place),

We

Modeling
the idea and form of a
poem requires paying close
attention to the original
poem.

Two
From Poem to Song

Paul Simon used Edwin Arlington Robinson's poem as the basis for a song. Read his version of the poem, noting similarities and differences.

Response notes

Richard Cory
Paul Simon

They say that Richard Cory owns one-half of this
    whole town,
With political connections to spread his wealth around.
Born into society, a banker's only child,
He had everything a man could want: power, grace and
    style.

But I work in his factory,
And I curse the life I'm living,
And I curse my poverty
And I wish that I could be
Richard Cory.

The papers print his picture almost everywhere he
    goes,
Richard Cory at the opera, Richard Cory at the show,
And the rumor of his parties, and the orgies on his
    yacht;
Oh, he surely must be happy with everything he's got.

But I work in his factory,
And I curse the life I'm living,
And I curse my poverty
And I wish that I could be
Richard Cory.

He freely gave to charity, he had the common touch,
And they were grateful for his patronage, and they
    thanked him very much.
So my mind is filled with wonder, when the evening
    headlines read:
"Richard Cory went home last night and put a bullet
    through his head."

But I work in his factory,
And I curse the life I'm living,
And I curse my poverty
And I wish that I could be
Richard Cory.

●◆In a group, discuss the differences between the song and the poem. Make a list of all the changes you noticed.

....

....

....

....

....

....

●◆Now go back to your modeled poem from the last lesson and adapt it to a song style. Write a four- or five-line refrain to insert after each stanza.

....

....

....

....

....

....

....

....

....

....

....

....

....

A ballad has a musical rhythm and a refrain that repeats a central idea.

Three
Writing a Sonnet

Sonnets can surprise you. They are traditionally written in **iambic pentameter**, the natural **rhythm** of English. Although they may not appear at first glance to be written in a highly structured meter, they are. Read Robert Frost's poem "Design" first just for the meaning. *Heal-all* in line two refers to a white wildflower common in New England meadows.

Response notes

Design
Robert Frost

a   I found a dimpled spider, fat and white,
b   On a white heal-all, holding up a moth
b   Like a white piece of rigid satin cloth—
a   Assorted characters of death and blight
a   Mixed ready to begin the morning right,
b   Like the ingredients of a witches' broth—
b   A snow-drop spider, a flower like a froth,
a   And dead wings carried like a paper kite.

a   What had that flower to do with being white,
c   The wayside blue and innocent heal-all?
a   What brought the kindred spider to that height,
a   Then steered the white moth thither in the night?
c   What but design of darkness to appall?—
c   If design govern in a thing so small.

●◆ Write a short paragraph describing the **tone** of this poem and how the rhythm, imagery, and diction affect the tone.

Frost's sonnet is of the type called **Italian**, which is characterized by two parts. The first, the octave, sets forth the situation or image in eight lines; the second, the sestet, then reflects on the meaning of what was presented in the first part. Look at Frost's poem to see how that holds up. Then summarize each part briefly in your own words.

Summary of the octave:

Summary of the sestet:

183

Now that you understand the basic structure of the sonnet, you are ready to write a word-for-word model or **emulation**:

1. Choose a subject you want to write about. It does not need to be related to Frost's at all.

2. Replace each major word (nouns, verbs, adjectives, and adverbs) of Frost's poem with a word of your own that serves the same grammatical purpose.

3. There are places where you can repeat the words of the original. Words such as *and*, *but*, and *or* may be kept; prepositions such as *in*, *out*, *above*, *through*, and *with* may be kept or replaced with other prepositions; and any form of the verb *to be* (*am*, *is*, *was*, *were*, and so on) may be used as in the original.

4. If you want to write a true sonnet, you need to follow the rhyme scheme that is listed by "Design." You may want to ignore the rhyming pattern and concentrate on the meaning.

•◦ Work in pencil so you can erase words if necessary.

after "Design" by Robert Frost

I found a dimpled spider, fat and white,

On a white heal-all, holding up a moth

Like a white piece of rigid satin cloth—

Assorted characters of death and blight

Mixed ready to begin the morning right,

Like the ingredients of a witches' broth—

A snow-drop spider, a flower like a froth,

And dead wings carried like a paper kite.

What had that flower to do with being white,

The wayside blue and innocent heal-all?

What brought the kindred spider to that height,

Then steered the white moth thither in the night?

What but design of darkness to appall?—

If design govern in a thing so small.

Word-for-word modeling is an exercise that helps a reader understand the skill of a poet.

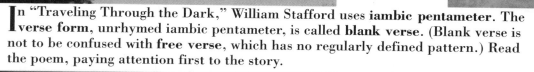

Four
Writing a Parallel Poem

In "Traveling Through the Dark," William Stafford uses **iambic pentameter**. The **verse form**, unrhymed iambic pentameter, is called **blank verse**. (Blank verse is not to be confused with **free verse**, which has no regularly defined pattern.) Read the poem, paying attention first to the story.

Response notes

Traveling Through the Dark
William Stafford

Traveling through the dark I found a deer
dead on the edge of the Wilson River road.
It is usually best to roll them into the canyon:
that road is narrow; to swerve might make more dead.

By glow of the tail-light I stumbled back of the car
and stood by the heap, a doe, a recent killing;
she had stiffened already, almost cold.
I dragged her off; she was large in the belly.

My fingers touching her side brought me the reason—
her side was warm; her fawn lay there waiting,
alive, still, never to be born.
Beside that mountain road I hesitated.

The car aimed ahead its lowered parking lights;
under the hood purred the steady engine.
I stood in the glare of the warm exhaust turning red;
around our group I could hear the wilderness listen.

I thought hard for us all—my only swerving—
then pushed her over the edge into the river.

185

How does the title contribute to its meaning? Who or what is traveling? Is there more than one traveler? How would you define the *dark* of the poem? Write down your initial impressions.

....

....

....

....

....

....

●◆Write a parallel poem by telling a story of your own in a manner similar to that of Stafford. Tell the story as if you are telling a friend about what happened. Present the situation and the choices, then explain which choice you made and why. You will have to be very economical in your word choice to do all this in a short poem. Reread Stafford's poem to see how he managed it.

1. Note a time when you had a hard decision to make.

2. List two possible choices you had and note what the outcome would be for each of the choices.

3. Write the storyline in two brief sentences.

4. What happened as a result of your choice? (This will be the reflective part of your poem.)

●◆ Now, using your notes, draft a poem.

Unrhymed iambic pentameter sounds like everyday speech. It is a meter commonly used in poetry because it is graceful but still simple.

Five Modeling and Drawing

Imagine that you have a camera that can take pictures not only of things but also of ideas. When you press the shutter, you capture the picture and also your thoughts. Read "Thirteen Ways of Looking at a Blackbird" by Wallace Stevens. Then next to each stanza, draw the scene that you envision from the words. You may need to look up a few words.

Response notes

Thirteen Ways of Looking at a Blackbird
Wallace Stevens

I

Among twenty snowy mountains,
The only moving thing
Was the eye of the blackbird.

II

I was of three minds,
Like a tree
In which there are three blackbirds.

III

The blackbird whirled in the autumn winds.
It was a small part of the pantomime.

IV

A man and woman
Are one.
A man and a woman and a blackbird
Are one.

V

I do not know which to prefer,
The beauty of inflections
Or the beauty of innuendoes,
The blackbird whistling
Or just after.

VI

Icicles filled the long window
With barbaric glass.
The shadow of the blackbird
Crossed it, to and fro.
The mood
Traced in the shadow
An indecipherable cause.

VII

O thin men of Haddam,
Why do you imagine golden birds?
Do you not see how the blackbird
Walked around the feet
Of the women about you?

VIII

I know noble accents
And lucid, inescapable rhythms;
But I know, too,
That the blackbird is involved
In what I know.

IX

When the blackbird flew out of sight,
It marked the edge
Of one of many circles.

X

At the sight of blackbirds
Flying in a green light,
Even the bawds of euphony
Would cry out sharply.

XI

He rode over Connecticut
In a glass coach.
Once, a fear pierced him,
In that he mistook
The shadow of his equipage
For blackbirds.

XII

The river is moving.
The blackbird must be flying.

XIII

It was evening all afternoon.
It was snowing
And it was going to snow.
The blackbird sat
In the cedar-limbs.

➥ Now write your own poem modeled after "Thirteen Ways of Looking at a Blackbird." First, select an object—not an abstraction, but a thing that you can see and touch. Draw five pictures of your subject, one in each of the boxes on the next page. Then, to the right of each framed picture, write a short mini-poem in the style of Stevens's stanzas. Title your poem "Five Ways of Looking at. . . ."

190

Drawing
can enhance the power of concrete images and
details in both reading and writing.

The Craft of Poetry

The craft of poetry may be compared to craft in other art forms. It is easy to see the results of craft when you look at a potter's work, for example. A crafted piece of pottery has shape and size. You have something to touch and look at. Some potters design their own glazes, achieving an effect that is highly personal. Other potters, such as the raku artists, follow the traditions for glazing and firing that potters have used for centuries.

A similar situation exists for poets. Some poets design their own forms, while others follow the traditional patterns of the old masters. The preference of poets for writing either free verse or fixed verse depends on many factors. Whatever the form, it is part of what we respond to.

When we read a poem, our first concern is always to create meaning from the ways that our experiences intersect with, reflect, or even challenge the ideas in the poem. Then we look more closely at form and how rhyme, rhythm, and stanza pattern affect our understanding.

One Organic Poetry

In "Poetics," A. R. Ammons addresses the question of how he goes about determining the **form** of a poem. In an essay, the poet Denise Levertov wrote, "For me, in back of the idea of organic form is the concept that there is a form in all things (and in our experience) that the poet can discover and reveal." Read Ammons's poem, marking in the response notes any questions and ideas.

Response notes

Poetics
A. R. Ammons

I look for the way
things will turn
out spiraling from a center,
the shape
things will take to come forth in

so that the birch tree white
touched black at branches
will stand out
wind-glittering
totally its apparent self:

I look for the forms
things want to come as

from what black wells of possibility,
how a thing will
unfold:

not the shape on paper—though
that, too—but the
uninterfering means on paper:

not so much looking for the shape
as being available
to any shape that may be
summoning itself
through me
from the self not mine but ours.

192

Discuss your ideas and questions with a partner or group. Look especially at the ending of the poem. What does Ammons mean by *ours* in the line "from the self not mine but ours"? Jot down your ideas about this last line.

Levertov could be describing Ammons's poem when she writes this about organic form: "content and form are in a state of dynamic interaction; the understanding of whether an experience is a linear sequence or a constellation raying out from and in to a central focus or axis, for instance, is discoverable only *in the work*, not before it."

●❖ Would you describe Ammons's poem as "a linear sequence" or "a constellation raying out"? What lines in the poem make you think it is one or the other? Write the relevant lines here and explain your choice.

●❖ Reread "Poetics." Then think about how Ammons's poem fits Levertov's definition of **organic form** in poetry. What do you think Ammons is trying to express through "Poetics"?

193

Organic
form arises
from a poet's
attempt to
record nature and
experience as
naturally as
possible.

Two

Reading Well

Dana Gioia, a poet who studied with Elizabeth Bishop, said that in her poetry class, "one did not interpret poetry; one experienced it. Showing us how to experience it clearly, intensely, and above all, directly was the substance of her teaching. One did not need a sophisticated theory. One needed only intelligence, intuition, and a good dictionary."

Try Bishop's approach on one of her own poems. Bring your intelligence, intuition, and a good dictionary to your reading of this poem. See what you make of it.

Response notes

194

One Art
Elizabeth Bishop

The art of losing isn't hard to master;
so many things seem filled with the intent
to be lost that their loss is no disaster.

Lose something every day. Accept the fluster
of lost door keys, the hour badly spent.
The art of losing isn't hard to master.

Then practice losing farther, losing faster:
places, and names, and where it was you meant
to travel. None of these will bring disaster.

I lost my mother's watch. And look! my last, or
next-to-last, of three loved houses went.
The art of losing isn't hard to master.

I lost two cities, lovely ones. And, vaster,
some realms I owned, two rivers, a continent.
I miss them, but it wasn't a disaster.

—Even losing you (the joking voice, a gesture
I love) I shan't have lied. It's evident
the art of losing's not too hard to master
though it may look like (*Write* it!) like disaster.

What do you think this poem is about?

●◆ Go back and reread the poem. This time, beside each stanza, list the items that the narrator "lost." How would you describe the progression of "lost" objects?

●◆ One of the features of poetry is repetition, whether of rhyming sounds, actual words, or even entire lines. Look specifically at the lines that are repeated, although with some variations. How do the changes in these lines affect your understanding of the poet's losses? (Look especially at the insertion of *Write* it!" in the last line.)

●◆ Reread your original thoughts about the meaning of "One Art." What, in your opinion, is Bishop saying in the poem?

Good readers of poetry rely on their intelligence, intuition, and a dictionary. Nothing else is necessary to enjoy poetry.

Three
Crafting a Villanelle

Theodore Roethke's "The Waking" is a **villanelle**, a complex traditional **verse form**. (Elizabeth Bishop's "One Art" was also one.) Read the poem first for what it says.

Response notes

The Waking
Theodore Roethke

a1
I wake to sleep, and take my waking slow.
I feel my fate in what I cannot fear.
a2
I learn by going where I have to go.

We think by feeling. What is there to know?
I hear my being dance from ear to ear.
a1
I wake to sleep, and take my waking slow.

Of those so close beside me, which are you?
God bless the Ground! I shall walk softly there,
a2
And learn by going where I have to go.

Light takes the Tree; but who can tell us how?
The lowly worm climbs up a winding stair;
a1
I wake to sleep, and take my waking slow.

Great Nature has another thing to do
To you and me; so take the lively air,
a2
And, lovely, learn by going where to go.

This shaking keeps me steady. I should know.
What falls away is always. And is near.
a1
I wake to sleep, and take my waking slow.
a2
I learn by going where I have to go.

196

The form of a villanelle is quite complex. The first (a1) and third (a2) lines are repeated each three times. The two lines repeat themselves alternately throughout the poem, coming together as a conclusion in the last **stanza** to make a four-line, rather than a three-line, end stanza. Notice that the first and third lines of each stanza **rhyme**, either exactly (*slow, go*) or with what is called a slant or half rhyme (*air, near*). Reread the poem and mark the **rhyme scheme** on the lines.

The rhythm of this poem is five **feet** per line, or **pentameter**. The villanelle may have any **rhythm**, as long as it is consistent. But the most common rhythms are **tetrameter** (four feet) or pentameter. One of the best ways to understand a fixed poetic form is to write one of your own.

➥Choose a subject for your own villanelle. The subject should be quite general, such as love or time. Write two sentences about your subject.

▶◆ Rewrite these two sentences so that they rhyme and have the same rhythm. These will be your repeating lines.

line 1:

line 3:

▶◆ Now, using the poems you have read as models, write your villanelle.

197

The villanelle has a tightly controlled form that enables poets to use repetition to build up ideas and emotions. By the last stanza, the two repeating lines mean more than they did at the beginning.

Four
Freeing the Verse Form

Creative writing teachers tell young poets not to make their poems sing-songy by writing every line in exactly the same kind of poetic **foot**. When the **rhythm** is too strict, readers start paying attention to the rhythm and forget to listen to the words. The title of Linda Pastan's poem refers to an introductory level college course (101) in prosody, the study of poetic **meter** and **verse forms**. Her memory of this course is the springboard for a poem that is as much about love as it is about prosody.

Response notes

Prosody 101
Linda Pastan

When they taught me that what mattered most
was not the strict iambic line goose-stepping
over the page but the variations
in that line and the tension produced
on the ear by the surprise of difference,
I understood yet didn't understand
exactly, until just now, years later
in spring, with the trees already lacy
and camellias blowsy with middle age,
I looked out and saw what a cold front had done
to the garden, sweeping in like common language,
unexpected in the sensuous
extravagance of a Maryland spring.
There was a dark edge around each flower
as if it had been outlined in ink
instead of frost, and the tension I felt
between the expected and actual
was like that time I came to you, ready
to say goodbye for good, for you had been
a cold front yourself lately, and as I walked in
you laughed and lifted me up in your arms
as if I too were lacy with spring
instead of middle aged like the camellias,
and I thought: so this is Poetry!

Look at the speaker of this poem. What is she like? Make up three **metaphors** for the speaker of the poem. You might compare her to an animal, a plant, one of the seasons, the kind of weather. When you have thought of your comparisons, write sentences that tell what she is like and why.

✒ The speaker is like:

1. .... *because she* ....

2. .... *because she* ....

3. .... *because she* ....

●◆ Use your comparisons in a description of the speaker of the poem. Tell what you know about her. Where does she live? Does she have a family? What are the most important things or people in her life?

....

....

....

....

●◆ Reread the poem. Notice how Pastan weaves the two subjects (poetry and love) together. Look at what the speaker says about love and about poetry. If you were asked to place this poem in an anthology, would you put it in a section of poems about love or a section of poems about poetry? Explain your decision.

....

....

....

199

....

....

....

....

....

....

....

....

....

....

....

The rhythm is one of a poet's most important tools for interesting the reader and emphasizing meaning.

Five The Idea of Poetry

You have read several poems that define poetry in an oblique way. They have indicated what poetry does, what it contains, and how it makes the writer feel.

➡️ Write a draft for a poem that contains your own original definition of poetry. Think about the place of images and concrete details in poetry. Think about the pattern that you wish to create. Be as serious or outlandish as you like—this is, after all, your definition.

Focus on the Writer: Toni Morrison

Toni Morrison was awarded the 1993 Nobel Prize in Literature. She was the first African American so honored. It was a sign of the importance of African American literature in the United States. Toni Morrison's stories probe the historical and mythic pasts of African Americans. Her characters seek to find their cultural identity in an environment of racial discrimination. As Morrison has said, "In the stories, I place the characters on a cliff. I push them as far as I can to see what they are made of. . . . I place them in the tragic mode so I can get at what those emotions really are."

In *The Bluest Eye* eleven-year-old Pecola Breedlove prays every night for blue eyes. In *Beloved*, Sethe escapes slavery only to have her experience haunt the lives of her children. In *Sula*, Joe Trace becomes a door-to-door cosmetic salesman in New York City after leaving a Virginia sharecropper's life. In each novel, Morrison's stories show how the larger world exerts forces and pressures on the individual. Her stories are intended, Morrison says, to illustrate "how and why we learn to live this life intensely and well."

One The Importance of Story

Toni Morrison was raised in an environment rich in **oral traditions**. "People told stories. Also there was the radio; I was a radio child. You get in the habit of gathering information that way, and imagining the rest. You make it up." In her Nobel Prize Lecture, Morrison suggests that narrative, the art and practice of storytelling, is a central way in which we learn about the world and ourselves.

← Response notes →

from **The Nobel Prize Lecture** by Toni Morrison

Narrative has never been merely entertainment for me. It is, I believe, one of the principal ways in which we absorb knowledge. I hope you will understand, then, why I begin these remarks with the opening phrase of what must be the oldest sentence in the world, and the earliest one we remember from childhood: "Once upon a time . . ."

"Once upon a time there was an old woman. Blind but wise." Or was it an old man? A guru, perhaps. Or a *griot* soothing restless children. I have heard this story, or one exactly like it, in the lore of several cultures.

"Once upon a time there was an old woman. Blind. Wise."

In the version I know the woman is the daughter of slaves, black, American, and lives alone in a small house outside of town. Her reputation for wisdom is without peer and without question. Among her people she is both the law and its transgression. The honor she is paid and the awe in which she is held reach beyond her neighborhood to places far away; to the city where the intelligence of rural prophets is the source of much amusement.

One day the woman is visited by some young people who seem to be bent on disproving her clairvoyance and showing her up for the fraud they believe she is. Their plan is simple: they enter her house and ask the one question the answer to which rides solely on her difference from them, a difference they regard as a profound disability: her blindness. They stand before her, and one of them says, "Old woman, I hold in my hand a bird. Tell me whether it is living or dead." She does not answer, and the question is repeated. "Is the bird I am holding living or dead?"

Still she does not answer. She is blind and cannot see her visitors, let alone what is in their hands. She does not know their color, gender or homeland. She only knows their motive.

The old woman's silence is so long, the young people have trouble holding their laughter.

Finally she speaks, and her voice is soft but stern. "I don't know," she says. "I don't know whether the bird you are holding is dead or alive, but what I do know is that it is in your hands. It is in your hands."

Her answer can be taken to mean: if it is dead, you have either found it that way or you have killed it. If it is alive, you can still kill it. Whether it is to stay alive is your decision. Whatever the case, it is your responsibility.

from **The Nobel Prize Lecture** by Toni Morrison

For parading their power and her helplessness, the young visitors are reprimanded, told they are responsible not only for the act of mockery but also for the small bundle of life sacrificed to achieve its aims. The blind woman shifts attention away from assertions of power to the instrument through which that power is exercised.

Speculation on what (other than its own frail body) that bird in the hand might signify has always been attractive to me, but especially so now, thinking as I have been about the work I do that has brought me to this company. So I choose to read the bird as language and the woman as a practiced writer.

Morrison tells a "Once Upon a Time" story—the story of the blind woman, the bird, and the young visitors—to illustrate what can be learned through story. She reinforces how the characters, actions, events, objects, and **setting** of a story represent many things. For example, as Morrison suggests, the "bird in the hand" can have several different meanings. Morrison chooses to "read the bird as language."

What is your interpretation of the story Morrison tells? What meaning does it have for you? Use a double-entry log to develop your interpretation. In the left column, jot characters, actions, events, objects, or phrases that are important to the story. In the right column, write a few words explaining what each means to you. What meaning, for example, do you make from the "blindness" of the storyteller? from the use of "Once Upon a Time"?

203

What's in the Story?	Meaning
Once Upon a Time	signals a story will be told
Blind Woman	ironic because she has insight

●❖ Write a short summary of the meaning of the story for you.

●❖ Now, select a story that has been important to you for one reason or another. Briefly retell the story. Then, write about the knowledge you gained from the story that might illustrate, as Morrison suggests, that story is "one of the principal ways in which we absorb knowledge."

The Story

Explanation of the importance of this story to my learning

A story can show the way a writer interprets the world.

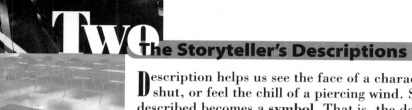

Two
The Storyteller's Descriptions

Description helps us see the face of a character, hear the sound of a door creaking shut, or feel the chill of a piercing wind. Sometimes, the object or person described becomes a **symbol**. That is, the description conveys meaning beyond the particular details. For example, Morrison means more by her title *The Bluest Eye* than a simple description of eye color.

.... from ***The Bluest Eye*** by Toni Morrison ....

Letting herself breathe easy now, Pecola covered her head with the ←—*Response notes*—→
quilt. The sick feeling, which she had tried to prevent by holding in
her stomach, came quickly in spite of her precaution. There surged in
her the desire to heave, but as always, she knew she would not.

"Please, God," she whispered into the palm of her hand. "Please
make me disappear." She squeezed her eyes shut. Little parts of her
body faded away. Now slowly, now with a rush. Slowly again. Her
fingers went, one by one; then her arms disappeared all the way to
the elbow. Her feet now. Yes, that was good. The legs all at once. It
was hardest above the thighs. She had to be real still and pull. Her
stomach would not go. But finally it, too, went away. Then her chest,
her neck. The face was hard, too. Almost done, almost. Only her tight,
tight eyes were left. They were always left.

Try as she might, she could never get her eyes to disappear. So
what was the point? They were everything. Everything was there, in
them. All of those pictures, all of those faces. She had long ago given
up the idea of running away to see new pictures, new faces, as
Sammy had so often done. He never took her, and he never thought
about his going ahead of time, so it was never planned. It wouldn't
have worked anyway. As long as she looked the way she did, as long
as she was ugly, she would have to stay with these people. Somehow
she belonged to them. Long hours she sat looking in the mirror, trying
to discover the secret of the ugliness, the ugliness that made her
ignored or despised at school, by teachers and classmates alike. She
was the only member of her class who sat alone at a double desk. The
first letter of her last name forced her to sit in the front of the room
always. But what about Marie Appolonaire? Marie was in front of her,
but she shared a desk with Luke Angelino. Her teachers had always
treated her this way. They tried never to glance at her, and called on
her only when everyone was required to respond. She also knew that
when one of the girls at school wanted to be particularly insulting to a
boy, or wanted to get an immediate response from him, she could say,
"Bobby loves Pecola Breedlove! Bobby loves Pecola Breedlove!" and
never fail to get peals of laughter from those in earshot, and mock
anger from the accused.

It had occurred to Pecola some time ago that if her eyes, those
eyes that held the pictures, and knew the sights—if those eyes of hers
were different, that is to say, beautiful, she herself would be different.

← Response notes →

Her teeth were good, and at least her nose was not big and flat like some of those who were thought so cute. If she looked different, beautiful, maybe Cholly would be different, and Mrs. Breedlove too. Maybe they'd say, "Why, look at pretty-eyed Pecola. We mustn't do bad things in front of those pretty eyes."

Pretty eyes. Pretty blue eyes. Big blue pretty eyes.
Run, Jip, run. Jip runs, Alice runs. Alice has blue eyes.
Jerry has blue eyes. Jerry runs. Alice runs. They run
with their blue eyes. Four blue eyes. Four pretty
blue eyes. Blue-sky eyes. Blue-like Mrs. Forrest's
blue blouse eyes. Morning-glory-blue-eyes.
Alice-and-Jerry-blue-storybook-eyes.

Each night, without fail, she prayed for blue eyes. Fervently, for a year she had prayed. Although somewhat discouraged, she was not without hope. To have something as wonderful as that happen would take a long, long time.

Thrown, in this way, into the binding conviction that only a miracle could relieve her, she would never know her beauty. She would see only what there was to see: the eyes of other people.

She walks down Garden Avenue to a small grocery store which sells penny candy. Three pennies are in her shoe—slipping back and forth between the sock and the inner sole. With each step she feels the painful press of the coins against her foot. A sweet, endurable, even cherished irritation, full of promise and delicate security. There is plenty of time to consider what to buy. Now, however, she moves down an avenue gently buffeted by the familiar and therefore loved images. The dandelions at the base of the telephone pole. Why, she wonders, do people call them weeds? She thought they were pretty. But grown-ups say, "Miss Dunion keeps her yard so nice. Not a dandelion anywhere." Hunkie women in black babushkas go into the fields with baskets to pull them up. But they do not want the yellow heads—only the jagged leaves. They make dandelion soup. Dandelion wine. Nobody loves the head of a dandelion. Maybe because they are so many, strong, and soon.

There was the sidewalk crack shaped like a Y, and the other one that lifted the concrete up from the dirt floor. Frequently her sloughing step had made her trip over that one. Skates would go well over this sidewalk—old it was, and smooth; it made the wheels glide evenly, with a mild whirr. The newly paved walks were bumpy and uncomfortable, and the sound of skate wheels on new walks was grating.

These and other inanimate things she saw and experienced. They were real to her. She knew them. They were the codes and touchstones of the world, capable of translation and possession. She owned the crack that made her stumble; she owned the clumps of dandelions whose white heads, last fall, she had blown away; whose yellow heads, this fall, she peered into. And owning them made her part of the world, and the world a part of her.

from *The Bluest Eye* by Toni Morrison

She climbs four wooden steps to the door of Yacobowski's Fresh Veg. Meat and Sundries Store. A bell tinkles as she opens it. Standing before the counter, she looks at the array of candies. All Mary Janes, she decides. Three for a penny. The resistant sweetness that breaks open at last to deliver peanut butter—the oil and salt which complement the sweet pull of caramel. A peal of anticipation unsettles her stomach.

She pulls off her shoe and takes out the three pennies. The gray head of Mr. Yacobowski looms up over the counter. He urges his eyes out of his thoughts to encounter her. Blue eyes. Blear-dropped. Slowly, like Indian summer moving imperceptibly toward fall, he looks toward her. Somewhere between retina and object, between vision and view, his eyes draw back, hesitate, and hover. At some fixed point in time and space he senses that he need not waste the effort of a glance. He does not see her, because for him there is nothing to see. How can a fifty-two-year-old white immigrant storekeeper with the taste of potatoes and beer in his mouth, his mind honed on the doe-eyed Virgin Mary, his sensibilities blunted by a permanent awareness of loss, *see* a little black girl? Nothing in his life even suggested that the feat was possible, not to say desirable or necessary.

"Yeah?"

She looks up at him and sees the vacuum where curiosity ought to lodge. And something more. The total absence of human recognition— the glazed separateness. She does not know what keeps his glance suspended. Perhaps because he is grown, or a man, and she a little girl. But she has seen interest, disgust, even anger in grown male eyes. Yet this vacuum is not new to her. It has an edge; somewhere in the bottom lid is the distaste. She has seen it lurking in the eyes of all white people. So. The distaste must be for her, her blackness. All things in her are flux and anticipation. But her blackness is static and dread. And it is the blackness that accounts for, that creates, the vacuum edged with distaste in white eyes.

Highlight or circle the various descriptions and references to eyes. Discuss with a partner what Pecola associates with blue eyes.

●◆ What do you think the eyes symbolize? How is this related to the title? Refer to examples from this excerpt to demonstrate your opinions.

◖◗ Write a description of a physical feature of your own that symbolizes some aspect of your personality or character. Through your description, emphasize how both you and others have defined you through this feature. Reread the excerpt to note some of the ways that you can use description to create a symbol.

Writers' descriptions of particular objects, characters, or events may lead a reader to see symbolic meaning beyond the particular details.

 **Writer as Social Commentator**

Morrison has said, "It would be a mistake to assume that writers are disconnected from social issues." She believes all good art examines the life of a community. A story grounds social issues in specific characters, places, actions, and beliefs. Read the following statements made by Morrison about *The Bluest Eye* and note the role Morrison defines for herself as a social commentator:

Response notes

"The impetus for writing *The Bluest Eye* in the first place was to write a book about a kind of person that was never in literature anywhere, never taken seriously by anybody—all those peripheral little girls. So I wanted to write a book that—if that child ever picked it up—would look representational."

"I began to write that book as a short story based on a conversation I had with a friend when I was a little girl. The conversation was about whether God existed; she said no and I said yes. She explained her reason for knowing that He did not: she had prayed every night for two years for blue eyes and didn't get them, and therefore He did not exist. What I later recollected was that I looked at her and imagined her having them and thought how awful that would be if she had gotten her prayer answered. I always thought she was beautiful. I began to write about a girl who wanted blue eyes and the horror of having that wish fulfilled."

"A metaphor is a way of seeing something, either familiar or unfamiliar, in a way that you can grasp it. If I get the right one, then I'm all right. But I can't just leap in with words, I have to get a hook. That's the way I think; I need it, the phrase or the picture or the word or some gesture."

Morrison stated in an interview that the story of Pecola illustrates how cultural beliefs have an effect on the individual's life. In interviews, Morrison has emphasized that her writing "will always be about the same thing—you know—about the whole world of Black people in this country."

●◆ Do you think it is important for a writer to critique society? Why or why not?

Many writers create their stories to expose or explore social issues. The stories are entertaining and compelling, but they also comment on the way we live.

Four

Structuring an Episode

The challenge of writing a scene is similar to juggling. A writer must get many stories "in the air" simultaneously. Interweaving or juggling thoughts and actions, interior and exterior talk, description and action helps readers experience in words what they often experience in life. Note how Morrison develops such a scene at the beginning of her third novel.

from *Song of Solomon* by Toni Morrison

⟵ *Response notes* ⟶

"You," she said, moving toward the stout woman. "Are these your children?"

The stout woman turned her head slowly, her eyebrows lifted at the carelessness of the address. Then, seeing where the voice came from, she lowered her brows and veiled her eyes.

"Ma'am?"

"Send one around back to the emergency office. Tell him to tell the guard to get over here quick. That boy there can go. That one." She pointed to a cat-eyed boy about five or six years old.

The stout woman slid her eyes down the nurse's finger and looked at the child she was pointing to.

"Guitar, ma'am."

"What?"

"Guitar."

The nurse gazed at the stout woman as though she had spoken Welsh. Then she closed her mouth, looked again at the cat-eyed boy, and lacing her fingers, spoke her next words very slowly to him.

"Listen. Go around to the back of the hospital to the guard's office. It will say 'Emergency Admissions' on the door, A-D-M-I-S-I-O-N-S. But the guard will be there. Tell him to get over here—on the double. Move now. Move!" She unlaced her fingers and made scooping motions with her hands, the palms pushing against the wintry air.

A man in a brown suit came toward her, puffing little white clouds of breath. "Fire truck's on its way. Get back inside. You'll freeze to death."

The nurse nodded.

"You left out a s, ma'am," the boy said. The North was new to him and he had just begun to learn he could speak up to white people. But she'd already gone, rubbing her arms against the cold.

"Granny, she left out a *s*."

"And a 'please.'"

"You reckon he'll jump?"

"A nutwagon do anything."

"Who is he?"

"Collects insurance. A nutwagon."

"Who is that lady singing?"

"That, baby, is the very last thing in pea-time." But she smiled when she looked at the singing woman, so the cat-eyed boy listened to the musical performance with at least as much interest as he devoted to the man flapping his wings on top of the hospital.

The crowd was beginning to be a little nervous now that the law was being called in. They each knew Mr. Smith. He came to their houses twice a month to collect one dollar and sixty-eight cents and write down on a little yellow card both the date and their eighty-four cents a week payment. They were always half a month or so behind, and talked endlessly to him about paying ahead—after they had a preliminary discussion about what he was doing back so soon anyway.

"You back in here already? Look like I just got rid of you."

"I'm tired of seeing your face. Really tired."

"I knew it. Soon's I get two dimes back to back, here you come. More regular than the reaper. Do Hoover know about you?"

They kidded him, abused him, told their children to tell him they were out or sick or gone to Pittsburgh. But they held on to those little yellow cards as though they meant something—laid them gently in the shoe box along with the rent receipts, marriage licenses, and expired factory identification badges. Mr. Smith smiled through it all, managing to keep his eyes focused almost the whole time on his customers' feet. He wore a business suit for his work, but his house was no better than theirs. He never had a woman that any of them knew about and said nothing in church but an occasional "Amen." He never beat anybody up and he wasn't seen after dark, so they thought he was probably a nice man. But he was heavily associated with illness and death, neither of which was distinguishable from the brown picture of the North Carolina Mutual Life Building on the back of their yellow cards. Jumping from the roof of Mercy was the most interesting thing he had done. None of them had suspected he had it in him. Just goes to show, they murmured to each other, you never really do know about people.

The singing woman quieted down and, humming the tune, walked through the crowd toward the rose-petal lady, who was still cradling her stomach.

"You should make yourself warm." she whispered to her, touching her lightly on the elbow. "A little bird'll be here with the morning."

"Oh?" said the rose-petal lady. "Tomorrow morning?"

'That's the only morning coming."

"It can't be," the rose-petal lady said. "It's too soon."

"No it ain't. Right on time."

The women were looking deep into each other's eyes when a loud roar went up from the crowd—a kind of wavy *oo* sound. Mr. Smith had lost his balance for a second, and was trying gallantly to hold on to a triangle of wood that jutted from the cupola. Immediately the singing woman began again:

O Sugarman done fly
O Sugarman done gone . . .

Downtown the firemen pulled on their greatcoats, but when they arrived at Mercy, Mr. Smith had seen the rose petals, heard the music, and leaped on into the air.

212

What techniques does Morrison employ to juggle the various stories in the scene? In the left column, list the separate stories that you find (Mr. Smith's, Guitar's, and so forth). Then, tell what you know about each of their stories.

Stories Within the Episode

Story	What the Story is About
Mr. Smith: fear, need to get away	
Guitar:	
North/South:	
Townspeople:	
The Rose-Petal Lady:	
The Singing Woman:	

Compare your chart with that of a partner. Discuss the following questions: how does Morrison structure the scene to include all the stories? What is the effect, on the reader, of telling several stories at once?

In order to reflect how we experience things, writers sometimes create scenes that tell several stories simultaneously.

Five Structuring Your Own Episode

Try structuring an episode of your own. First, think of an incident that you would like to tell. List two or three characters involved and some of the highlights of each character's individual story. You will want to narrate aspects of the experience through a combination of thought and action.

Character	The Story and Details
Character #1	
Character #2	
Character #3	

•❖ Write a short scene in which you interweave the stories of each character into some larger event (as the story of Mr. Smith does) that brings them all together in one place.

Combining different facets of experience—thought, action, and multiple points of view—is one way of structuring an episode to bring immediacy to the scene.

Poetry Workshop

Talking About Poetry

To talk and to write about poems, you need to understand some of the terms used to describe them.

RHYTHM Recurrent sound in poetry is called rhythm. A poem can have a regular or irregular rhythm. The rhythm of a regular poem is referred to as meter.

METER The pattern of stressed and unstressed syllables in a line of poetry is called meter.

LINE Poetry is broken into lines that contain a varying number of words. Metrical lines are broken into units called feet and referred to by the number of feet:

- monometer: a line having one foot
- dimeter: a line having two feet
- trimeter: a line having three feet
- tetrameter: a line having four feet
- pentameter: a line having five feet
- hexameter: a line having six feet

FOOT The basic unit of a metrical line is the foot. It is a combination of two or three stressed and unstressed syllables. The basic feet are the following:

- iamb: an unstressed syllable followed by a stressed syllable (examples: "below," "He ought")
- trochee: a stressed syllable followed by an unstressed syllable (examples: "falling," "grown-up")
- anapest: two unstressed syllables followed by a stressed syllable (examples: "intervene," "through the air")
- dactyl: a stressed syllable followed by two unstressed syllables (examples: "yesterday," "A is for")
- spondee: two stressed syllables (examples: "daybreak," "knock, knock")

215

RHYME The similarity or likeness of sound between two words is called rhyme. *Sat* and *cat* are a perfect rhyme because the vowel sounds and the final consonant of each word match exactly. Rhymes in which these do not exactly match (for example, *room/storm* or *chill/fell*) are known as half-rhymes.

End rhyme (rhyme between the last word of two lines of poetry) is the most common in English, but there are many examples of internal rhyme (rhyme between words in a single line).

STANZA A group of lines that are set off to form a division in a poem is called a stanza. A stanza roughly makes up a unit of thought. In a metrical poem, the first stanza should set the pattern of the rhythm and rhyme. A two-line stanza is called a couplet. A three-line stanza is a tercet. A four-line stanza is called a quatrain.

Understanding the Rhyme

To determine the rhyme scheme of a poem (or stanza), underline the last word of each line. Use a small letter *a* to mark the sound of the first line. Every end word that has that sound will be an *a*. Use *b* for the next rhyming end word that has a different sound. Below, the rhyme scheme is marked on the opening lines of "Design" by Robert Frost (see page 182) as an example.

> I found a dimpled spider, fat and <u>white</u>,   a
> On a white heal-all, holding up a <u>moth</u>   b
> Like a white piece of rigid satin <u>cloth</u>—   b
> Assorted characters of death and <u>blight</u>   a
> Mixed ready to begin the morning <u>right</u>,   a

Understanding Rhythm in Poetry

One of the most important but also most difficult things to do when studying poetry is to hear the rhythm of a poem. It is important because it is one of the best ways to understand the poet's art. It is difficult because scanning lines—that is, determining where the stresses fall and what the meter of the line is—takes a lot of practice.

The first thing to remember is that poetry is an oral art. Stresses are determined by how a poem is read aloud. Robert Frost wrote in one of his letters, "The ear does it. The ear is the only true writer and the only true reader." Read the following lines from Frost's "Design" aloud and concentrate on the rhythm.

> What had that flower to do with being white,
> The wayside blue and innocent heal-all?
> What brought the kindred spider to that height,
> Then steered the white moth thither in the night?

The lines above are in iambic pentameter. The second and third lines are almost perfectly metrical. Below, the stressed syllables on the second line are marked by a / and unstressed ones by a ˘.

> ˘   /   /   /   ˘   /   ˘   /   /   /
> | The way | side blue | and in | no cent | heal-all |

The meter of this is iambic, but not every foot is an iamb. The second and fifth feet are spondees. Spondaic substitution is very common in lines of iambic pentameter.

Poets vary the meter to stress words or ideas and to keep the rhythm from growing boring. Note the substitution in the last foot of the following line:

```
  ˘      /      ˘   /    ˘   /    ˘  /   /  /
| What brought | the kin | dred spi | der to | that height |
```

Frost uses the first and last feet to maintain the iambic pattern but puts great stress on the words "kindred spider." It emphasizes Frost's theme in the poem, the relationship between all things.

When you want to figure out the meter of a poem, begin by breaking a line into feet to determine the length. Then try to figure out the basic metrical foot of the line. One of the most important clues in scanning is verse form. Many poems are written in traditional verse forms that follow certain rules for the meter.

Recognizing Verse Forms

Some of the common verse forms in English are:

BLANK VERSE a verse form consisting of unrhymed iambic pentameter lines. It is the verse form closest to spoken English. Shakespeare's dramas were mostly written in blank verse. (See pages 185, 198.)

COUPLET two lines of poetry with the same meter that often rhyme. "I am his Highness' dog at Kew; / Pray tell me, Sir, whose dog are you?" (Alexander Pope)

FREE VERSE poetry without any regular rhythm. (See pages 11, 134.)

LIMERICK a five-line stanza usually rhyming *aabba*, with the first, second, and fifth lines written in trimeter and the third and fourth in dimeter. The limerick is generally witty and nonsensical.

SONNET a poem consisting of 14 lines of iambic pentameter. It is one of the most popular verse forms in English. There are two main types of sonnets, distinguished by the rhyme schemes and structure: the Italian sonnet and the Shakespearean sonnet.

- Italian sonnet (also known as the Petrarchan), a 14-line poem broken into two parts—an octave (eight lines) and a sestet (six lines)—usually rhyming *abbaabba cdecde*. The general structure of an Italian sonnet is to present a question or situation in the octave that is then resolved or commented on in the sestet. (See page 182.)

- Shakesperean sonnet (also known as the Elizabethan), a 14-line poem consisting of three quatrains and a final couplet. The rhyme scheme is *abab cdcd efef gg*. Usually, the quatrains set forth a question or conflict that is answered or resolved in the couplet. (See page 10.)

VILLANELLE a complex and highly-musical verse form that consists of five tercets rhyming *aba*, with a final quatrain rhyming *abaa*. The first line is used again as the sixth, twelfth, and eigtheenth lines. The third line is used again as the ninth, fifteenth, and nineteenth lines. (See pages 194, 196.)

Glossary

abstract, existing only as an idea, condition, or feeling that cannot be seen, heard, or touched. Something that is abstract is not CONCRETE.

alliteration, the repetition of the same initial sound in two or more nearby words in poetry or prose. "When to the sessions of sweet silent thought." (William Shakespeare, Sonnet 30) (See ASSONANCE and CONSONANCE.)

allusion, a reference in a literary work to a familiar person, place, or thing.

annotation, a note or comment added to a text to question, explain, or critique the text.

antithesis, a FIGURE OF SPEECH that uses an opposition or contrast of ideas for effect. "It was the best of times, it was the worst of times...." (Dickens, *A Tale of Two Cities*)

archetype, a SYMBOL, story pattern, THEME, or character type that appears often in literature or art. Archetypes have a universal significance and recognizability. Two archetypal characters are the knight undertaking a dangerous quest and the damsel in distress.

argument, the ideas or reasoning that holds together a work of literature. Argument is generally used in discussion of short poems, particularly the SONNET.

assonance, the repetition of the same vowel sounds in two or more nearby words in poetry or prose. It is similar to ALLITERATION, but not confined to the initial sound in a word. "That dolphin-torn, that gong-tormented sea." (W. B. Yeats, "Byzantium") (See CONSONANCE.)

audience, those people who read or hear what an author has written.

autobiography, an author's account of his or her own life. (See BIOGRAPHY and MEMOIR.)

biography, the story of a person's life written by another person. (See AUTOBIOGRAPHY.)

blank verse*, a VERSE FORM consisting of unrhymed iambic pentameter lines. It is the verse form closest to spoken English. Most of Shakespeare's dramas were written in blank verse. (See RHYME.)

central idea, see MAIN IDEA.

characterization, the method an author uses to describe characters and their personalities.

concrete, existing as an actual object that can be seen, heard, or touched. Something that is concrete is not ABSTRACT.

consonance, the repetition of the same consonant sound before or after different vowels in two or more nearby words in poetry or prose. It is similar to ALLITERATION, but not confined to the initial sound in a word. "Courage was mine, and I had mystery / Wisdom was mine, and I had mastery." (Wilfred Owen, "Strange Meeting") (See ASSONANCE.)

couplet*, two LINES of poetry with the same METER and which often RHYME. "I am his Highness' dog at Kew; / Pray tell me, Sir, whose dog are you?" (Alexander Pope)

description, writing that paints a colorful picture of a person, place, thing, or idea using CONCRETE, vivid DETAILS.

detail, words from a DESCRIPTION that convince the AUDIENCE, explain a process, or in some way support the MAIN IDEA. Details are generally vivid, colorful, and appeal to the senses.

dialect, a form of speech characteristic of a class or region and differing from standard speech in pronunciation, vocabulary, and grammatical form. The imitation of this regional speech in literature requires the use of altered, phonetic spellings.

dialogue, conversation carried on by the characters in a literary work.

diction, an author's choice of words in a literary work.

digression, the presentation of material that is not part of the PLOT or main THEME in a literary work.

dimeter*, one of the metric lines of poetry. A LINE with two feet is in dimeter. (See METER and FOOT.)

emulation, a copy or IMITATION of a piece of literature, done to practice and study the style of the original's author.

essay, a type of NONFICTION in which ideas on a single topic are explained, argued, and described. It is an immensely varied FORM.

fact, a thing known to be true or to have actually happened. (See OPINION.)

fiction, PROSE writing that tells an imaginary story. (See NOVEL and SHORT STORY.)

figurative language, language used to create a special effect or feeling. It is characterized by FIGURES OF SPEECH or language that compares, exaggerates, or means something other than what it first appears to mean.

figures of speech, literary devices used to create

218

* See Poetry Workshop (pages 215–217)

special effects or feelings by making comparisons. The most common types are ALLITERATION, ANTITHESIS, HYPERBOLE, METAPHOR, METONYMY, PERSONIFICATION, REPETITION, SIMILE, and UNDERSTATEMENT.

first-person narrator, See POINT OF VIEW.

flashback, a scene or episode in FICTION, POETRY, or DRAMA that goes back to an earlier time in the story to explain the present situation.

foot*, the basic unit of METER. It is a combination of two or three stressed and unstressed syllables. The most common feet are the IAMB and the TROCHEE. (See STRESS.)

foreshadowing, hints about what is going to happen, given by the writer to the reader.

form, the structure or organization a writer uses for a literary work. There are a large number of possible forms, including fable, parable, romance, PARODY, and so on. (See VERSE FORM.)

free verse*, poetry that does not have a regular METER or a RHYME scheme.

generalization, an idea or statement that emphasizes the general characteristics rather than the specific details of a subject.

genre, a category or type of literature based on its style, form, and content. The major genres are FICTION, NONFICTION, drama, and POETRY.

gothic, literature characterized by supernatural or sensational happenings—creating a mysterious and sometimes frightening story.

hexameter*, one of the metric lines of poetry. A LINE with six feet is in hexameter. (See METER and FOOT.)

hyperbole, a FIGURE OF SPEECH that uses exaggeration, or overstatement, for effect. "I have seen this river so wide it had only one bank." (Mark Twain, *Life on the Mississippi*)

iamb*, a metrical FOOT in poetry. It consists of an unstressed syllable followed by a stressed one. *New York* and *repeat* are examples of iambs. (See METER and STRESS.)

imagery, the words or phrases a writer uses to represent objects, feelings, actions, or ideas. Imagery is usually based on sensory DETAILS.

imitation, a piece of literature consciously modeled after an earlier piece. An imitation can a be copy done for practice or a serious homage to a writer. (See EMULATION.)

inference, a reasonable conclusion about a character or event in a literary work drawn from the limited facts made available.

inflection, a change in the tone or the pitch of the voice. The inflection of the voice implies the use of a word. The word *well* can be used as an adjective, noun, or exclamation and is inflected differently with each use.

irony, the use of a word or phrase to mean the exact opposite of its literal or normal meaning.

Italian sonnet* (also known as the Petrarchan), a 14-LINE poem broken into two parts—an octave (eight lines) and a sestet (six lines)—usually rhyming *abbaabba cdecde*. The general structure of an Italian sonnet is to present a question in the octave that is then resolved in the sestet. (See RHYME and SONNET.)

journal, a daily record of thoughts, impressions, and autobiographical information. A journal can be a source of ideas for writing.

limited narrator, a THIRD-PERSON NARRATOR who is telling a story from one character's POINT OF VIEW. (See OMNISCIENT NARRATOR.)

line*, the metric form of POETRY, which is generally distinguished from PROSE by being broken into lines. Lines are named according to the number of feet they contain and the pattern of these feet. The principal line lengths are MONOMETER, DIMETER, TRIMETER, TETRAMETER, PENTAMETER, and HEXAMETER. (See METER and FOOT.)

literal, the actual or dictionary meaning of a word. It also refers to the common meaning of phrases, rather than the imaginative or implied meaning an author may add.

local color, the use of the speech, setting, and customs of a particular region of the country in FICTION, POETRY, or drama.

main idea, the central point or purpose in a work of literature. It is often stated in a thesis statement or topic sentence. Main idea is more commonly employed in discussing NONFICTION than the other GENRES.

memoir, a type of AUTOBIOGRAPHY. Memoir generally focuses on a specific subject or period rather than the complete story of the author's life.

metaphor, a FIGURE OF SPEECH in which one thing is described in terms of another. The comparison is usually indirect, unlike a SIMILE in which it is direct. "My thoughts are sheep, which I both guide and serve." (Sir Philip Sidney, *Arcadia*)

meter*, the pattern of stressed and unstressed syllables in a LINE of poetry. The basic unit of meter is the FOOT. (See STRESS.)

219

metonymy, a FIGURE OF SPEECH that substitutes one word for another that is closely related. "The White House has decided to provide a million more public service jobs" is an example. *White House* is substituting for *president*.

monometer*, one of the metric lines of poetry. A LINE with one FOOT is in monometer. (See METER.)

mood, the feeling a piece of literature arouses in the reader. It is reflected by the overall atmosphere of the work. (See TONE.)

myth, a traditional story connected with the beliefs of a culture.

narrative, writing or speaking that tells a story or recounts an event.

narrator, the person telling the story in a work of literature. (See LIMITED NARRATOR, OMNISCIENT NARRATOR, and POINT OF VIEW.)

nonfiction, PROSE writing that tells a true story. There are many categories of nonfiction, including AUTOBIOGRAPHY, BIOGRAPHY, and ESSAY. (See GENRE.)

novel, a lengthy fictional story with a plot that is revealed by the speech, action, and thoughts of the characters. Novels differ from SHORT STORIES by being developed in much greater depth and detail. (See FICTION and GENRE.)

objective, NONFICTION writing that relates information in an impersonal manner; without feelings or opinions. (See SUBJECTIVE)

omniscient narrator, a THIRD-PERSON NARRATOR who is able to see into the minds of all the characters in a literary work, narrating the story from multiple POINTS OF VIEW. (See LIMITED NARRATOR.)

opinion, what one thinks or believes. An opinion is based on knowledge, but it is not a FACT.

oral literature, stories composed orally or made up as the author goes along. This is the oldest form of literature and is characterized by REPETITION, patterns, and fluidity. Poetic forms such as the ballad and the epic originated as oral literature.

organic form*, the form of a poem that derives from the nature of the subject and theme rather than arbitrarily chosen rules and conventions. Organic poetry favors open forms like BLANK VERSE and the QUATRAIN rather than fixed forms like the SONNET or VILLANELLE. The idea behind organic form is that a poem develops like a living organism.

parody, a form of literature intended to mock a particular literary work or style. It is meant to be humorous.

pentameter*, one of the metric lines of poetry. A LINE with five feet is in pentameter. (See METER and FOOT.)

personification, a FIGURE OF SPEECH in which an author embodies an inanimate object with human characteristics. "The rock stubbornly refused to move" is an example.

perspective, See POINT OF VIEW.

plot, the action or sequence of events in a story. It is usually a series of related incidents that build upon one another as the story develops.

poetry*, a GENRE of writing that is an imaginative response to experience reflecting a keen awareness of language. Poetry is generally characterized by LINES, RHYTHM and, often, RHYME.

point of view, the angles or perspective from which a story is told. In the first-person point of view, the story is told by one of the characters: "I was tired so I took the shortcut through the cemetery." In the third-person point of view, the story is told by someone outside the story: "The simple fact is that he lacked confidence. He would rather do something he wasn't that crazy about doing than risk looking foolish." A third-person narrator can be LIMITED or OMNISCIENT. (See NARRATOR.)

prose, writing or speaking in the usual or ordinary form. Prose is any writing that is not POETRY.

quatrain*, a STANZA of four LINES. The lines can be in any METER or RHYME scheme.

repetition, a FIGURE OF SPEECH in which a word, phrase, or idea is repeated for emphasis and rhythmic effect in a piece of literature. "Bavarian gentians, big and dark, only dark / darkening the day-time, torch-like with the smoking blueness of Pluto's gloom." (D. H. Lawrence, "Bavarian Gentians")

rhyme*, the similarity or likeness of sound existing between two words. *Sat* and *cat* are a perfect rhyme because the vowel sounds and final consonant of each word match exactly. Rhyme is a characteristic of POETRY.

rhythm*, the ordered occurrence of sound in POETRY. Regular rhythm is called METER. Poetry without regular rhythm is called FREE VERSE.

scene, See SETTING.

setting, the time and place in which the action of a literary work occurs.

220

Shakespearean sonnet* (also known as the Elizabethan), a 14-LINE poem consisting of three QUATRAINS and a final COUPLET. The rhyme scheme is *abab cdcd efef gg*. Usually, the quatrains set forth a question or conflict that is resolved in the couplet. (See RHYME and SONNET.)

short story, a brief fictional story. It usually contains one major theme and one major character. (See FICTION, GENRE, and NOVEL.)

simile, a FIGURE OF SPEECH in which one thing is likened to another. It is a direct comparison employing the words *like* or *as*. Cicero's "A room without books is like a body without a soul" is an example. (See METAPHOR.)

slang, word uses that are not part of the formal language, but carry a particular vividness or coloring. Slang words appear and fade with great speed.

sonnet*, a poem consisting of 14 LINES of iambic pentameter. It is one of the most popular VERSE FORMS in English. There are two main types of sonnets distinguished by their RHYME schemes and structure: the ITALIAN SONNET and the SHAKESPEAREAN SONNET.

stanza*, a group of LINES that are set off to form a division in POETRY. A two-line stanza is called a COUPLET. A four-line stanza is a QUATRAIN.

stream of consciousness, a style of writing in which a character's thoughts and feelings are recorded as they occur. Images, memories, and ideas occur in a seemingly random fashion as the writer tries to imitate the way people perceive things.

stress*, the vocal emphasis given a syllable or word in a metrical pattern. (See METER.)

structure, See FORM.

style, how an author uses words, phrases, and sentences to form ideas. Style consists of the qualities and characteristics that distinguish one writer's work from another's.

subjective, NONFICTION writing that includes personal feelings, attitudes, or OPINIONS. (See OBJECTIVE.)

symbol, a person, place, thing, or event used to represent something else. The *dove* is a symbol of peace. Characters in literature are often symbolic of an idea.

syntax, sentence structure. It is the order and relationship of words in a sentence.

tetrameter*, one of the metric lines of poetry. A LINE with four feet is in tetrameter. (See METER and FOOT.)

theme, the statements about life that a writer is trying to get across in a piece of writing (lengthy pieces may have several themes). In more complex literature, the theme is implied.

thesis, a statement of purpose, intent, or MAIN IDEA in a literary work.

third-person narrator, See POINT OF VIEW.

tone, a writer's attitude toward the subject. A writer's tone can be serious, sarcastic, solemn, OBJECTIVE, and so on.

tradition, the inherited past that is available to an author to study and learn from. This generally includes language, the body of literature, FORMS, and conventions.

trimeter*, one of the metric lines of poetry. A LINE with three feet is in trimeter. (See METER and FOOT.)

trochee*, a metrical FOOT in poetry. It consists of a stressed syllable followed by an unstressed one. *Falling* and *older* are examples of trochees. (See METER and STRESS.)

understatement, a FIGURE OF SPEECH that states an idea with restraint to emphasize what is being written about. The common usage of "Not bad" to mean *good* is an example of understatement.

verse form*, the form taken by the lines of a poem. Some of the common verse forms in English are the SONNET, BLANK VERSE, the COUPLET, and the QUATRAIN. (See LINE.)

vignette, in literature, a short, vivid description or sketch.

villanelle*, a complex and highly-musical verse form that consists of five tercets rhyming *aba*, with a final quatrain rhyming *abaa*. The first line is used again as the sixth, twelfth, and eigtheenth lines. The third line is used again as the ninth, fifteenth, and nineteenth lines.

voice, an author's distinctive style and unique way of expressing ideas.

221

10 "To a Friend Whose Work Has Come to Triumph" from *All My Pretty Ones* by Anne Sexton. Copyright © 1962 by Anne Sexton, renewed 1990 by Linda G. Sexton. Reprinted by permission of Houghton Mifflin Company. All rights reserved.

11 "The Starry Night" from *All My Pretty Ones* by Anne Sexton. Copyright © 1962 by Anne Sexton, renewed 1990 by Linda G. Sexton. Reprinted by permission of Houghton Mifflin Company. All rights reserved.

18 Excerpt from "A Friendship Remembered" by Maxine Kumin from *Anne Sexton: The Artist and Her Critics*, edited by J. D. McClatchy. Published by Indiana University Press, 1978. Reprinted by permission of J. D. McClatchy.

19 "The Fury of Overshoes" from *The Death Notebooks* by Anne Sexton. Copyright © 1974 by Anne Sexton. Reprinted by permission of Houghton Mifflin Company. All rights reserved.

22 Excerpt from *Middle Passage* by Charles Johnson. Copyright © 1990 Charles Johnson. Reprinted with the permission of Scribner, a Division of Simon & Schuster.

24, 26 Excerpt from *The Way to Rainy Mountain* by N. Scott Momaday. Reprinted by permission of University of New Mexico Press.

28 Excerpt from *How the García Girls Lost Their Accents* by Julia Alvarez. Copyright © 1991 by Julia Alvarez. Published by Plume, an imprint of Dutton Signet, a division of Penguin Putnam. Originally published in hardcover by Algonquin Books of Chapel Hill. Reprinted by permission of Susan Bergholz Literary Services, New York. All rights reserved.

31 Excerpt from "How to Tell a True War Story" from *The Things They Carried* by Tim O'Brien. Copyright © by Tim O'Brien. Reprinted by permission of Houghton Mifflin Company/Seymour Lawrence. All rights reserved.

34, 36, 37 Excerpt from *Young Men and Fire* by Norman Maclean. Published by the University of Chicago Press. Copyright © 1992 by the University of Chicago. All rights reserved.

37 Quotation from *Conversations with Capote* by Lawrence Grobel. Copyright © 1985 by Lawrence Grobel. Foreward copyright © 1985 by James A. Michener. Used by permission of Dutton Signet, a division of Penguin Putnam Inc.

39, 41 Excerpt from *The Perfect Storm* by Sebastian Junger. Copyright © 1997 by Sebastian Junger. Reprinted by permission of W. W. Norton & Company, Inc.

44 "Ahead of the Night" by Ernie Pyle. Reprinted by permission of Scripps Howard Foundation.

48 Excerpt from *Rolling Nowhere* by Ted Conover. Copyright © 1981, 1984 by Ted Conover. Used by permission of Viking Penguin, a division of Penguin Putnam Inc.

51 Excerpt from *The Pilgrim at Tinker Creek* by Annie Dillard. Copyright © 1974 by Annie Dillard. Reprinted by permission of Annie Dillard and Blanche C. Gregory, Inc.

53 "Square Space" by Jon Roush. Originally appeared in *The San Francisco Examiner Magazine*, Sunday, October 30, 1994. Copyright © 1994 by Jon Roush. Reprinted by permission of the author.

58 Excerpt from "America and I" from *How I Found America: Collected Stories of Anzia Yezierska*. Copyright © 1991 by Louise Levitas Henriksen. Reprinted by permission of Persea Books, Inc.

59 "Ellis Island" by Joseph Bruchac from *This Remembered Earth,* edited by Geary Hobson, Albuquerque: Red Earth Press, 1979.

62 "Translated from the American" by Sherman Alexie from *Old Shirts and New Skins*. Copyright © Regents of the University of California. Reprinted by permission of the American Indian Studies Center, UCLA.

64 "next to of course god america I" by E. E. Cummings. Copyright © 1926, 1954, 1991 by the Trustees for the E. E. Cummings Trust. Copyright © 1985 by George James Firmage, from *Complete Poems 1904–1962* by E. E. Cummings, edited by George J. Firmage. Reprinted by permission of Liveright Publishing Corporation.

66 Excerpt from "Where the Kissing Never Stops" from *Slouching Towards Bethlehem* by Joan Didion. Copyright © 1966, 1968 and renewed 1996 by Joan Didion. Reprinted by permission of Farrar, Straus & Giroux, Inc.

70 "Dust of Snow" by Robert Frost from *The Poetry of Robert Frost*, edited by Edward Connery Lathem, Copyright © 1936, 1951 by Robert Frost, 1964 by Lesley Frost Ballantine. Copyright © 1923, 1969 by Henry Holt and Company, Inc. Copyright © 1997 by Edward Connery Lathem. Reprinted by permission of Henry Holt and Company, Inc.

72 "Black Rook in Rainy Weather," from *The Colossus* by Sylvia Plath. Copyright © 1960 by Sylvia Plath. Permission of the author's estate and William Heinemann, Ltd.

75 "Otherwise" from *Otherwise: New and Selected Poems* by Jane Kenyon. Copyright © 1996 by the Estate of Jane Kenyon. Reprinted with the permission of Graywolf Press, Saint Paul, Minnesota.

77 "Auto Wreck" by Karl Shapiro. Copyright © 1941, 1987 by Karl Shapiro. Reprinted by arrangement with Wieser & Wieser, Inc.

79 "Study of Two Pears" from *Collected Poems* by Wallace Stevens. Copyright © 1942 by Wallace Stevens and Renewed ©1970 by Holly Stevens. Reprinted by permission of Alfred A. Knopf, Inc.

82 "Sisyphus" from *Poems 1930-1960* by Josephine Miles. Reprinted by permission of Indiana University Press

84 "The Mountain" from *The Triumph of Achilles* by Louise Glück. Copyright © 1985 by Louise Glück. Reprinted by permission of The Ecco Press.

88 "Dog's Death" from *Midpoint and Other Poems* by John Updike. Copyright © 1969 by John Updike. Reprinted by permission of Alfred A. Knopf, Inc.

90 "The Great Blue Heron" from *Mermaids in the Basement* © 1984 by Carolyn Kizer. Reprinted by permission of: Copper Canyon Press, P.O. Box 271, Port Townsend, WA 98368.

93 Truman Capote in conversation with Gerald Clarke, June 1984. Quoted from the frontispiece of *Capote: A Biography* by Gerald Clarke, published by Simon & Schuster, 1988. Used by permission of The Truman Capote Literary Trust.

94 Quotation from *Truman Capote* by George Plimpton. Copyright © 1998 by George Plimpton. Used by permission of Doubleday, a division of Bantam Doubleday Dell Publishing Group, Inc.

94 "Louis Armstrong" by Truman Capote. Copyright © 1957 by Truman Capote and Richard Avedon. Reprinted with the permission of Simon & Schuster from *Observations* by Truman Capote and Richard Avedon.

96 "Miriam" from *The Selected Writings of Truman Capote*. Copyright © 1945, renewed 1973 by Conde Nast Publications, Inc. Reprinted by permission of Random House, Inc.

112 "My Father Sits in the Dark" from *My Father Sits in the Dark and Other Stories* by Jerome Weidman. Copyright © 1934 by Jerome Weidman. Copyright renewed 1961 by Jerome Weidman. Reprinted by permission of Brandt & Brandt Literary Agents, Inc.

117 Excerpt from *Cold Mountain* by Charles Frazier. Copyright © 1997 by Charles Frazier. Used by permission of Grove/Atlantic, Inc.

119 "The End of Something" from *In Our Time* by Ernest Hemingway. Copyright © 1925 Charles Scribner's Sons. Copyright renewed 1953 by Ernest Hemingway. Reprinted with permission of Scribner, a Division of Simon & Schuster.

125 Excerpt from *Notes of a Native Son* by James Baldwin. Copyright © 1955, renewed 1983 by James Baldwin. Reprinted by permission of Beacon Press, Boston.

128 Excerpt from *The Invisible Thread* by Yoshiko Uchida. Copyright © 1991 Yoshiko Uchida. Reprinted with the permission of Simon & Schuster Books for Young Readers, an imprint of Simon & Schuster Children's Publishing Division.

222

131 Excerpt from *Farewell to Manzanar* by James D. Houston and Jeanne Wakatsuki Houston. Copyright © 1973 by James D. Houston. Reprinted by permission of Houghton Mifflin Company. All rights reserved.

134 "In Response to Executive Order 9066" from *Crossing With the Light* by Dwight Okita (Tia Chucha Press, Chicago). Copyright © 1992. Used by permission of the author.

136 "Shikata Ga Nai" from *The Winters of That Country: Tales of the Man-Made Seasons* by John Sanford. Copyright © 1984 by John Sanford. Reprinted with the permission of Black Sparrow Press.

138 Excerpt from *Snow Falling on Cedars* by David Guterson. Copyright © 1994 by David Guterson. Reprinted by permission of Harcourt Brace & Company.

142 "A Lady's Beaded Bag" from *The Collected Stories of Tennessee Williams*. Copyright © 1948 by Tennessee Williams. Reprinted by permission of New Directions Publishing Corp.

147 Excerpt from "Flying Home" from *Flying Home and Other Stories* by Ralph Ellison. Copyright © 1996 by Fanny Ellison. Reprinted by permission of Random House, Inc.

150 "The Far and the Near" from *From Death to Morning* by Thomas Wolfe. Copyright 1935 by Charles Scribner's Sons. Copyright renewed © 1963 by Paul Gitlin Administrator C.T.A. Reprinted with permission of Scribner, a Division of Simon & Schuster.

156 "I, Too, Sing America" from *Collected Poems* by Langston Hughes. Copyright © 1994 by the Estate of Langston Hughes. Reprinted by permission of Alfred A. Knopf, Inc.

160 "One of the Seven Has Somewhat to Say" by Sara Henderson Hay. Copyright © 1982 by Sara Henderson Hay. Reprinted by permission of the University of Arkansas Press.

162 "This Is Just to Say" from *Collected Poems 1909–1939, Volume 1* by William Carlos Williams. Copyright © 1938 by New Directions Publishing Corp. Reprinted by permission of New Directions Publishing Corp.

163 "Variations on a Theme by William Carlos Williams" from *Thank You and Other Poems* by Kenneth Koch. Copyright © 1962, 1985 by Kenneth Koch. Reprinted with permission of the author.

166 "Penelope" from *The Portable Dorothy Parker*. Copyright © 1928, renewed 1956 by Dorothy Parker. Introduction by Brendan Gill. Used by permission of Viking Penguin, a division of Penguin Putnam Inc.

168 "An Ancient Gesture" from *Collected Poems* by Edna St. Vincent Millay. Copyright © 1954 by Norma Millay Ellis. All rights reserved. Reprinted by permission of Elizabeth Barnett, literary executor.

170 "Siren Song" from "You are Happy" by Margaret Atwood © 1974 by Margaret Atwood, currently found in *Selected Poetry 1965-1975* by Houghton Mifflin. Reprinted with permission of the author.

173 "Demeter's Prayer to Hades" by Rita Dove. Copyright © 1992 by Rita Dove. Reprinted from *Poetry*, October 1992 by permission of the author.

175 "Myth" from *A Muriel Rukeyser Reader*. Published 1994 by W. W. Norton, NYC. Copyright © William L. Rukeyser.

178 "Richard Cory" from *The Children of the Night* by Edwin Arlington Robinson (New York: Charles Scribner's Sons, 1897).

180 "Richard Cory" by Paul Simon. Copyright © 1966 Paul Simon. Used by permission of Paul Simon Music.

182 "Design" by Robert Frost from *The Poetry of Robert Frost*, edited by Edward Connery Lathem, Copyright © 1936, 1951 by Robert Frost, 1964 by Lesley Frost Ballantine. Copyright © 1923, 1969 by Henry Holt and Company, Inc. Copyright © 1997 by Edward Connery Lathem. Reprinted by permission of Henry Holt and Company, Inc.

185 "Traveling through the Dark" from *The Way It Is: New and Selected Poems* by William Stafford. Copyright © 1998 by the Estate of William Stafford. Reprinted with the permission of Graywolf Press, Saint Paul, Minnesota.

188 "Thirteen Ways of Looking at a Blackbird" from *Collected Poems* by Wallace Stevens. Copyright © 1942 by Wallace Stevens. Renewed ©1970 by Holly Stevens. Reprinted by permission of Alfred A. Knopf, Inc.

192 "Poetics" from *The Selected Poems, Expanded Edition* by A. R. Ammons. Copyright © 1969 by A. R. Ammons. Reprinted by permission of W. W. Norton & Company, Inc.

193 Quotation from Dana Gioia. Copyright © 1986 by Dana Gioia. Reprinted by permission. Originally published in *The New Yorker*. All rights reserved.

193 "One Art" from *The Complete Poems 1927–1979* by Elizabeth Bishop. Copyright © 1979, 1983 by Alice Helen Methfessel. Reprinted by permission of Farrar, Strauss & Giroux, Inc.

196 "The Waking" from *The Collected Poems of Theodore Roethke*. Copyright © 1953 by Theodore Roethke. Used by permission of Doubleday, a division of Bantam Doubleday Dell Publishing Group, Inc.

198 "Prosody 101" from *A Fraction of Darkness* by Linda Pastan. Copyright © 1983 by Linda Pastan. Reprinted by permission of W. W. Norton & Company. Inc.

202 Excerpt from The Nobel Prize Lecture by Toni Morrision. Copyright © 1993 The Nobel Foundation, Knopf. Reprinted by permission of International Creative Management, Inc.

205 Excerpt from *The Bluest Eye* by Toni Morrison. Copyright © 1970 by Henry Holt. Reprinted by permission of International Creative Management, Inc.

209 Reprinted by permission of International Creative Management, Inc. Copyright © 1994 Toni Morrison.

211 Excerpt from *Song of Solomon* by Toni Morrison. Copyright © 1977 by Alfred A. Knopf, Inc. Reprinted by permission of International Creative Management, Inc.

Every effort has been made to secure complete rights and permissions for each literary excerpt presented herein. Updated acknowledgments will appear in subsequent printings.

223

Design: Christine Ronan Design

Photographs: Unless otherwise noted below, all photographs are the copyrighted work of Mel Hill.

Front and Back cover: Copyright © Richard H. Johnson/FPG International

9 Copyright © Jean Francois Gate/Tony Stone Images

21 Copyright © Swapan Parekh/Black Star

33 Copyright © Bruce Coleman Inc.

43 Copyright © Peter Brown/Peter Brown

57 Copyright © Library of Congress/Corbis

69 Copyright © Jane Gifford/Tony Stone Images

81 Copyright © James Harrington/Tony Stone Images

93 Copyright © Frank Saragnese/FPG International

111 Copyright © David Turnley/Black Star

127 Copyright © Wayne Levin/FPG International

141 Copyright © SuperStock International

155 Copyright © Vicki Ragan/Vicki Ragan

165 Copyright © Barbara Maurer/Tony Stone Images

177 Copyright © Marc Carter/Gamma Liason International

191 Copyright © Ron Coppock/Gamma Liason International

201 Copyright © Thomas Hoepker/Magnum Photos

Picture Research: Feldman and Associates